Co... Y0-CDD-519

Eng. Portion JOB TEV 560P
ABS-1974-50,000-Q-1-04626

INTRODUCTION

This devotional guide was written in response to the new translation in Today's English Version of the Book of Job "JOB FOR MODERN MAN" published by the American Bible Society. It is a translation that clearly opens the book's themes, drama, and structure for today's reader. The meditations and the new translation are printed together for your convenience. To receive the greatest value read the section from Job listed under the title before reading the meditation.

Beginning with chapter three, the Book of Job takes the form of a drama, with the major characters, Job, Eliphaz, Bildad, Zophar, and Elihu in dialogue as they struggle to explain the suffering of Job. The first question, as in our own experience of pain, is, "Why?" As this question is explored the characters in the drama are driven to seek the answer to a larger question: "When and how does man find peace and an enduring relationship with his Creator?"

The meditations in *My Servant Job* are designed to apply some of the deep meaning of the Book of Job to our daily needs and problems. The Lord speaks of Job as "my servant Job" in chapter 1:3. Job struggles to be the Lord's servant in times of prosperity and health and in times of loss and physical suffering, The story of Job is the story of every person whom the Lord names "my servant" by the call to faith in Jesus Christ.

Vernon R. Schreiber

iv

OUR COMMON CONDITION
Job 1.1-5

There was a man named Job, who lived in the land of Uz. He worshiped God and was faithful to him. He was a good man, careful not to do anything evil (1.1).

Have you ever known a person who apparently leads a busy and comfortable life in which just about everything in the world of business or career, in the sphere of family life, and in the realm of religion seems well in hand? Perhaps I am talking about you! I know I am talking about a man named Job.

Have you ever known an extremely upright and conscientious person who nevertheless has had all kinds of trouble come his way? Has that acquaintance indicated that his greatest torment does not lie in the nature of the tragedy which has visited him, but in the nagging suspicion that God is no longer listening to him? Again, I may be talking about you. Certainly this is the story of Job.

In fact, we are all a part of the human condition that leads us to ask at one time or another, "Why, God? Why?" That is why we can all profit from the Book of Job. The Book of Job will not give us quick and easy answers, but it definitely can become the school of the Holy Spirit through which we will be led to cherish this mighty promise of God: "Before they call, I will answer, and while they are yet speaking, I will hear" (Isaiah 65.24 RSV).

Welcome to this study of Job!

O Father, your holy Word is the schoolroom of life for me. Send your Spirit to be my teacher! Amen.

WOULD YOU STILL BELIEVE?

Job 1.6-12

"Would Job worship you if he got nothing out of it?" (1.9).

Have you seen someone sitting in a hospital, or perhaps being wheeled into church, and thought, "If that happened to me, would I still believe?"

This is the question behind the opening chapters of the Book of Job. In a most dramatic setting God and Satan confront one another. This confrontation is followed by the suffering of Job. I must confess that no matter how I try to explain, or explain away, this mystifying agreement, I still have no final answer as to why trouble comes. We only know that in this life there is trouble, and hand in hand with that trouble there is the temptation to fall away from God.

The tests of life, for us and for Job, will always be with us. The nature of some of those tests may make us wonder, "Would I still believe in God if it came to *that*?" The fact is, we will never know the answer in advance, at least not in terms of our own human strength. Even as we think the question, the only answer lies in an act of faith, a faith which will grow, God promises, *as it is tested*. Are we at this moment wondering about tomorrow? The Lord reassuringly says, "As your days, so shall your strength be" (Deuteronomy 33.25b RSV).

O God, at those times when the very foundations of my life are shaken, strengthen me with the assurance that you will still be with me. Amen.

DON'T BLAME GOD
Job 1.13-22

In spite of everything that had happened, Job did not sin by blaming God (1.22).

Sometimes tragedy strikes in incredible ways. I think of the occasion when a family lost its home in a fire. A compassionate motel owner provided them with shelter. Then two of their boys, disregarding the warning of an employee, drowned in the motel's swimming pool.

Such was one day in the life of Job. It dawned with his heart gladdened by the thought of his children happily gathered at the home of one of the elder brothers. Then the world began to fall apart. He is told of the loss of his flocks. A second messenger reports that a great storm has twisted out of the desert and killed all his children.

His reply, "The Lord gave and now he has taken away" has been quoted so often that we might think that it simply rolled off his tongue, even as we hear it glibly quoted by some would-be comforter or philosopher of our own day. In fact, grief had dealt Job a terrible blow. He withdrew from his companions. He tore his clothes, shaved his head, and hurled himself down on the ground. Only then did faith speak out from the midst of a bereaved parent's terrible anguish: "The Lord gave, and now he has taken away. May his name be praised!" (1.21).

O God, life is hard at times, but I pray that you would keep me from ever blaming you! Amen.

NO HELP FROM HOME
Job 2.1-10

"Why don't you curse God and die?" (2.9).

External calamity is one thing. The ravaging of your very own body is quite another. This becomes the next step in Job's suffering. His disfigurement is so complete that only a garbage dump can serve as a suitable backdrop for his miserable appearance. There he sits and picks his scabs.

Who will stand by a person in a moment like this? I think of the theme song from *High Noon,* "Do not forsake me, O my darling, on this our wedding day." A man wants his wife to stand by him. But it does not always happen that way. We can only guess as to whether his wife's tone of voice indicates that she simply does not want Job around any more or whether she is only wishing for a merciful end to his misery. In any event, her suggestion that he "curse God and die" is of no help at all.

While we should not go through life anticipating such disappointments, on the other hand we know that it was out of such a real experience that the Psalmist once wrote, "My father and mother may abandon me, but the Lord will take care of me" (Psalm 27.10 TEV). Job's spirit is sustained by this God-based security as he answers, "You are talking nonsense! When God sends us something good we welcome it. How can we complain when he sends us trouble?" (2.10).

Thank you, Lord, for my family. Make us instruments of hope to one another through our trust in you. Amen.

THE COMFORT OF SILENCE
Job 2.1-13

Then they sat there on the ground with him for seven days and nights without saying a word (2.13a).

You and I live in a world saturated with voices seeking to convince us of what we should accept, try, believe, or just plain swallow. Advice and exhortations come at us from every side. Therefore we are conditioned to believe that when someone needs comfort, we ought to *say* something. If we feel that we cannot say it, then we send a card. We do not believe that our mere nearness, or a simple light touch can mean more to a suffering friend than a whole fusillade of words.

In comparison to our insensitivity to what people are really looking for, we must give Job's friends credit for a good beginning, at least. At the outset they showed their compassion by sitting on the ground with him for seven days and nights without saying a word. They knew he needed their presence and their time, not their words. In fact, it was not until Job's friends began to open their mouths that they began making mistakes.

In our hurried age we would do well to remember that true compassion always consists of more than a spate of words. It includes our presence. May the Spirit of Jesus lead us to the side of those who suffer, demonstrating the love of God.

Lord Jesus, in my times of trouble you are with me. Lead me now to those who need me. Amen.

OUR FEELINGS OF ANGER
Job 3.1-26

God, put a curse on the day I was born (3.2a).

We have all witnessed someone taking a bad piece of news about death or illness with what appears to be great serenity. Sometimes it seems as if they have not heard a word that was said. Perhaps they haven't! The mind often blots out the full impact of the truth.

Then the shock wears off. It is followed by a feeling of anger which is not unlike that of Job, who, in his frustration, wishes that God would put a curse on the day he was born and feels that even death would be better than life (3.20-26).

Such anger usually shocks us. We do not like to see it emerge, either in ourselves or in others. We consider it to be one of those feelings which call for stern self-examination. What, then, should be our response? Should we rebuke ourselves or others by saying, "What's wrong with you? This isn't like you at all! Where is your faith?"

There is a better way. It goes beyond either excusing or condemning anger. That way takes us to the cross and to an awareness that expressions of anger are frequently a signal that someone is suffering a great deal and needs understanding, not a scolding. Before the cross of Christ we can spill out our feelings and then let the pardoning love of God give a new and positive direction to our lives.

Father, let the blessing of your love rest upon all my days. Amen.

OUR FEELINGS OF GUILT
Job 4.1—5.27

Man brings trouble on himself, as surely as sparks fly up from a fire (5.7).

Have you heard someone diagnose another's misfortune in these terms, "Well, in *my* opinion, God must be punishing him for something we don't know about!"? I have. I hear Eliphaz speaking in this vein in his first reply to Job. He is arguing that Job must make amends and do the things which will make up for his guilt before God.

There is an element of truth in his advice, "Happy is the person whom God corrects! Do not resent it when he reprimands you" (5.17, cf. Prov. 3.11). However, his question, "Can a man be right in the sight of God? Can anyone be pure before his Creator?" (4.17) should also be a reminder that even our sincerest repentance will never be of such high quality that *we* will have set things right with God.

Eliphaz's approach is dangerously misleading if it leads to the conclusion that we are able, through proper repentance, to make up for our guilt before God. It can also lead to worse despair if the trouble does not go away. "Have I still not done enough?" the sinner asks. "Am I still not right with God?" Such an emphasis forgets the miraculous message that Christ died for the world at the very height of its unworthiness.

Show me my guilt and then take me beyond it, O Lord. Take me to the cross of Jesus. Amen.

PLUNGED INTO DESPAIR
Job 6.1-30

God has lined up his terrors against me (6.4b).

In the case history of Job we are looking at a typical sequence of reactions to trouble. First there is shock, then anger, then charges of guilt. The next step is also a common one. Job falls into a state of deep depression. He says, "Almighty God has shot me with arrows, and their poison spreads through my body" (6.4a). Life is a tasteless thing in his mouth. He compares the usefulness of his friends to that of those mountain streams which are roaring torrents in the springtime when the snow is melting, but dry and barren in the summer when you need them the most (6.15-17). He gives up and says that he wishes God would go ahead and kill him (6.9-10).

The expression of such feelings should not surprise us or shock us. Despair is often a part of our inner turmoil in the time of continuing trouble. But we do not need to be permanent captives of such feelings. The moment when we feel pressed down by despair is exactly the time when the light of God's love, shining from the cross of Christ, can penetrate our darkness. The Christ who suffered for us will never leave us alone.

Father, I am often lost in a maze of confused and bitter feelings. Help me to remember that triumphant faith is never instantaneous, but always the product of genuine struggle. Amen.

OUR FEAR OF HONESTY
Job 7.1-21

Why use me for your target practice? Am I that big a burden to you? (7.20b).

Years ago a very wise woman gave me a new outlook toward the Scriptures when she said, "I love the Psalms, don't you? Those men are not afraid to ask the question, 'Why?' " This is a different and deeper approach than that of most people. They expect religious thoughts and biblical quotations to be cast in the form of sugar-sweet platitudes. They become extremely uncomfortable when they hear a man of God laying bare his heart in an honest expression of his feelings.

The ferocious attacks on the part of Job's friends suggests to me that they were afraid to listen to an honest expression of his feelings. They felt threatened by his frank assessment of his terrible condition.

What about our reaction to others as they pour out their feelings? Are we afraid to listen to them because they might be recognized as our own as well? If so, then let us take heart by remembering the human side to all of our Lord's sufferings: "In the days of his flesh, Jesus offered up prayers and supplications, *with loud cries and tears*" (Hebrews 5.7a RSV).

Dear Father, as I think of the Bible's cries, shouts and prayers by people just like myself, give me both the courage to ask the question, "Why?" plus the openness to accept the answers you give. Amen.

OUR SPIRIT OF JUDGMENT
Job 8.1-22

"Reeds can't grow where there is no water; . . . Godless men are like those reeds" (8.11a,13a).

We all know how people are tempted to pass judgment on others. Sometimes they will even suggest their sufferings and troubles are all due to some evil that they must have done. Bildad seems to be unsurpassed in this technique. He calls Job a windbag. He says that Job's children deserved their death as just punishment from God (8.1-4). His premise is that just as "reeds can't grow where there is no water," so suffering exists only where it is deserved as repayment for previous acts of wickedness (8.11-13).

Have we stopped to consider how this kind of self-righteous reasoning can add to a friend's misery? Such a spirit of judgment can result in the tragic consequence that we actually block out someone else's way to heartfelt repentance. Instead of helping, we have only set in motion the mechanisms of self-justification as the voice of *our* judgment drowns out the authentic voice of God.

Hearing the voice of God in both his judgment and mercy, we are equipped to speak to one another so that together we will be ready to hear the Son of God saying, "Neither do I condemn thee. Go and sin no more."

Lord, help me to perceive the limits of my ability to judge others who are suffering, and expand instead the boundaries of my love and understanding. Amen.

OUR TIMES OF BEWILDERMENT
Job 9.1-24

God gave the world to the wicked. He made all the judges blind. And if God didn't do it, who did? (9.24).

In Archibald MacLeish's modern drama about Job, Nickles mocks "J.B." by saying,
> If God is God, he is not good.
> If God is good, he is not God.

Such questions can arise within any of us. Certainly it was a part of Job's problem. While he does not want to deny the eternal power of God, he honestly cannot see any moral justification for God's actions. Why should he be suffering so much? His doubts are expressed in the poignant words, "God passes by, but I cannot see him. . . . Nothing matters; innocent or guilty, God will destroy us" (9.11,22b).

Instead of condemning Job out of hand, we should seek to understand him—and thus ourselves. Don't we all long for that revelation of God which will finally silence the cry, "I can't see him!"?

There is one way to discover the goodness of God and see him at last. The gospel bids us to behold Jesus who, though oppressed and afflicted, "like a lamb that is led to the slaughter . . . opened not his mouth" (Isaiah 53.7 RSV). As strange as it may scem, the stinging thorns, the heavy lash, the rough iron nails piercing his hands are signs that God reigns and is good; for through his Son he has drawn our suffering and sorrow upon himself.

Thank you, Jesus, that my frustration is turned into serenity as I turn my eyes to you and find that I see the face of God. Amen.

11

OUR LONGING FOR A MEDIATOR
Job 9.25—10.22

If God were human I could answer him back; we could go to court to decide our quarrel. But there is no one to step between us—no one to judge both God and me (9.32-33).

One of man's deepest desires is to have a friend who can step between almighty God and himself and establish peace again. Job says that he knows of no way that this can be done, but how he longs for just such a solution!

What Job so desperately desires has now been given to us—a mediator. "There is one mediator between God and men, the man Christ Jesus" (1 Timothy 2.5b RSV). As we of the "new age" of Christ read the Old Testament, we know that what matters in the court of God is not the brilliant defense we can present concerning our guilt or innocence. What is supremely important is the fact that the long-awaited mediator now stands by our side. In the language of the courtroom, "If any one does sin, we have an advocate with the Father, Jesus Christ the righteous; and he is the expiation for our sins, and not for ours only but also for the sins of the whole world" (1 John 2.1b-2 RSV). What a case the crucified Lord can plead! He pleads it for us!

It's true, O Lord, that I needmeoto stand up for me. I praise your name that this fr end is already there. Amen.

INFURIATING CONCEIT
Job 11.1-20

God knows which men are worthless; he sees all their evil deeds (11.11).

In the coming days God's Word will be leading us to think about "the fallen." However, we must watch out for the attitude with which we use that loaded phrase. For instance, Zophar, friend number three, has put Job in that category; and it is with great delight that he sets out to give Job a real verbal scourging. He even goes so far as to say, "God is punishing you less than you deserve" (11.6b).

It is difficult to imagine a more insensitive remark than Zophar's glib promise to Job: "All your troubles will fade from your memory" (11.16a). Does he really think that Job will forget his children's death that easily? Then Zophar goes on to conclude that he himself must be good because he is not suffering and that Job must be evil because he is suffering. He asserts, "God knows which men are worthless." That kind of conceit only repels people; and it is a stench in the nostrils of God because it confuses the judgment of men with the judgment of God.

God knows the hearts of all men. He does not need any of us to be another Zophar. So let us leave it that way. Let us speak to a "fallen" friend in such a way that together we will hear God's voice of judgment and then be ready for his promise of mercy.

Heavenly Father, deliver me from conceit, that I might neither drive others away from a sense of your grace nor lose it myself. Amen.

YOUR WISDOM IS A FALSEHOOD
Job 12.1-25

Yes, you are the voice of the people. When you die, wisdom will die with you (12.1-2).

If you would be a successful speaker in matters of religion, here is a time-tested formula. Tell your listeners that they, continuing in the way of righteousness, will go ever onward and upward. Reassure them that those whom they see suffering have brought it upon themselves. This was Zophar's approach, and I have the feeling that if he lived today, he could gain a large following, either from the pulpit or from the political platform.

Job in his suffering knows that life is not as simple as Zophar would make it out to be. He is engaged in more than verbal retaliation when he gives his answer in chapter 12. He draws attention to the mystifying ways of God in the events of history: "Old men have wisdom, but God has wisdom and power. . . . Drought comes when God withholds rain; floods come when he turns water loose. . . . He destroys the wisdom of rulers, and makes leaders act like fools. . . . He makes nations strong and great, but then he defeats and destroys them" (12.12-13,15,17,23). Although we do not usually describe him as such, Job is carrying out the role of a true prophet as he challenges Zophar's neat little system; and in the long run it is this honesty which catches the ear of the people who have lost their hold on God.

God, send us prophets who do not tell us what we want to hear but what we need to hear, including the reminder that every minute we must depend on your grace alone. Amen.

THE LONGINGS OF THE LOST
Job 13.1-28

I'm nothing but a leaf... a dry piece of straw.... I crumble like rotten wood, like a moth-eaten coat (13.25,28).

These words from the lips of Job remind us of Martin Luther who once remarked that if we were required to stand alone before the holy God for only a moment, we would shrivel up like a leaf thrown into a fire. He would have easily understood the despairing words coming from the heart of Job.

Not everyone who is unable to turn to God in the midst of trouble is necessarily stubborn or arrogant. It may be that their despair has become complete because they have tried so desperately to fathom the mystery of evil and suffering. Their protest is a part of their search. That is why they cannot swallow any religious palliative which merely commends "thinking positively" as the sure remedy for every situation, or settle for any other easy answer.

Jesus always had his greatest impact on such seekers. They sensed that he was a man who had made his own search and knew what he was talking about when he said, "Blessed are those who hunger and thirst for righteousness, for they shall be satisfied" (Matthew 5.6 RSV).

Don't despair, Jesus tells us. The presence of God is not a blast furnace. Those who take up his cross and follow him will find that it becomes the ground for true peace.

I'm hungry, Lord, and so are others. Feed us. Fill us. Lead us. Through you God's love can be found. Amen.

BELIEVING AGAIN
Job 14.1-22

But I will wait for better times . . . Then you will call and I will answer (14.14-15).

We like to speak of faith being like a brightly burning torch in the midst of darkness, but often it is more like a tiny flame set in a drafty corner. It rises for a moment, flickers, wanes, seems to be completely dead, and then shows itself again.

At this point the fire of Job's faith is almost out as he speaks about how a tree which has been cut down has a chance for new life where man has none (14.7-10). Then there follows a flicker of hope. A remembrance of God's love fills his mind and he exclaims, "Then you will watch every step I take, but you will not keep track of my sins. You will forgive my sins and put them away; you will wipe out all the wrongs I have done" (14.16-17).

This outburst of hope is like a wave striking the shore and then receding again. No sooner has he spoken than Job lapses back into gloom (14.18-22). But is this so unusual for the human spirit? Perhaps this is a proper moment for all of us to remember that it is not the splendidly consistent quality of faith that saves anyone. What is important is that we, though we feel just as weak as Job did, keep on reaching out to the God who has promised, "a bruised reed he will not break, and a dimly burning wick he will not quench" (Isaiah 42.3a RSV).

Dear Father, by the remembrance of the love and mercy of your Son, keep the flame of my faith still burning. Amen.

GAMES WE DON'T NEED TO PLAY
Job 15.1—16.5

Empty words, Job! . . . A wicked man who oppresses others will be in trouble as long as he lives. . . . That is the fate of the man who shakes his fist at God (15.1,20,25a).

For several days we have been stressing the harmful effect of a judgmental spirit. Today we see Eliphaz at work with absolutely no intention of letting up on Job. He sounds so righteous! The accused appears to be so wicked! But is Eliphaz really helping? Job's reply says that he is not: "If you were in my place and I in yours, I could say everything you are saying" (16.4a).

However, our real problem is not to choose sides between Job and Eliphaz. We need to recognize that neither Job, nor Eliphaz, nor any one of us is free from sin. God's word of judgment stands over against all of us, not just "the other guy." There is no room for trying to deny our own guilt or for seeking to feel at least a little bit better by proving that someone else is more sinful than we are.

Christ's death for sinners has removed the need for playing games of fault finding so let's stop playing them! Instead, let us find our peace in the good news that God's grace is wide enough to contain the infinite guilt of all men.

Help me, Lord, to walk where others have walked, not that I might condone sin, but that I might understand people and thus become a fitting ambassador for the life you now offer. Amen.

WITHOUT HOPE, IF NOT FOR GOD
Job 16.6—17.16

I want someone to plead with God for me, as a man pleads for his friend (16.21).

Job's mind seems to be divided as to whether he will be vindicated by God or rebuked, but one thing he knows: he needs a friend to give him help. We cannot calculate the exact meaning in Job's mind as he says, "There is someone in heaven to stand up for me and take my side. I want God to see my tears and hear my prayer" (16.19-20). However, in the age of the New Testament this yearning should stir in us a new appreciation of the hope now delivered to us: "Who is to condemn? Is it Christ Jesus, who died, yes, who was raised from the dead, who is at the right hand of God, who indeed intercedes for us?" (Romans 8.34 RSV).

If we could *not* say this, then we too would have to admit, " . . . the grave is my father, and the worms that eat me are my mother and sisters. Where is there any hope for me? . . . Hope will not go with me when I go to the world of the dead" (17.14-16).

Our inner assurance does not come from within us, nor from the absence of trouble in our lives, but from the experience of Jesus in our hearts. He makes us able to say, "If God is for us, who is against us? He who did not spare his own Son but gave him up for us all, will he not also give us all things with him?" (Romans 8.31b-32 RSV).

Thank you God for the hope Christ Jesus always gives me. Amen.

DO ACCUSERS DISCOURAGE YOU?
Job 18.1—19.29

In this body I will see God (19.26b).

Job's comforters, including Bildad, who try to terrorize Job by describing how the wicked will be "dragged off to face King Death" (18.14b), are of no comfort at all. But perhaps therein lies their greatest value! They are forcing Job to find his own source of strength, and out of despair arises the great passage, 19.25-27.

What is the full meaning of his answer? Is it an expression of the hope of the resurrection as older translations seem to suggest? Or is Job simply rising to a new height of faith in believing that God will still be his deliverer from this loathsome disease? In either case, we are seeing how the Spirit of God can lead a man, and can lead us as well, through the depths of despair to the kind of hope that only God can create.

We all have our own accusers who, like Eliphaz, Zophar, and Bildad, would tell us that there is no reason for us to hope in God, no reason to believe that at the end of time God will vindicate those who believe in him. It is true that such accusations can create terror. On the other hand, they can strengthen in us that faith which says, "I know whom I have believed, and I am sure that he is able to guard until that Day what has been entrusted to me" (2 Timothy 1.12b RSV).

Dear God, I'm waiting for you. I know you will come. Amen.

SOWING AND REAPING
Job 20.1-29

No wicked man has been happy for long (20.5).

How would you like it if a life-long friend suddenly seemed to have as his one ambition in life the goal of convincing you that the reason for your suffering lay in some great and unconfessed wickedness on your part? This seems to be Zophar's intent as he says, among other things, "Job, you upset me.... Surely you know that from ancient times, when man was first placed on earth, no wicked man has been happy for long.... All his wealth will be destroyed in the flood of God's anger" (20.1,4-5,28).

The trouble with Job's friends is not that they are speaking no truth at all, but that they know only half-truths. On the one hand, the Bible clearly says, "Whatever a man sows, that he will also reap" (Galatians 6.7b RSV). The history of mankind also shows us how God can be seen "trampling out the vintage where the grapes of wrath are stored."

But the answer we need cannot be found in this part of the truth alone. What we need to remember is that God's just wrath, which we cannot deny, has been revealed in order to point us to his mercy. From out of the depths of that mercy God has sent to us his Son, Jesus Christ. By his death on the cross that Son, in the total sense of the words, has reaped what we have sown. Thank God for that!

O God, if I have forgotten the seeds of destruction which I have sown, then wake me up to both your wrath and mercy! Amen.

THE REAL ROAD TO PEACE
Job 21.1-34

*Why does God let evil men grow old and prosper?
(21.7).*

I wonder if we have been tempted to agree with
the substance of Job's reply to Zophar as we find it
in chapter 21: The wicked get away with everything, while the good suffer for their faithfulness.
All of us can understand the feelings of the Psalmist: "It is for your sake that we are being killed all
the time, that we are treated like sheep to be
slaughtered. Wake up, Lord! Why are you asleep?
Get up! Don't reject us forever!" (Psalm 44:22-23
TEV).

The friends of Job suggest that in the face of such
feelings, the only way to peace is through abject
self-condemnation. They are wrong. Job seems to
believe that he will find peace through total self-
vindication. *He* is wrong. We shall not find peace
through either of these approaches.

"He [Christ] is our peace!" (Ephesians 2.14a
RSV). Christ Jesus is the source of that true and
lasting peace which the world longs for but will
never find apart from him. The testimony of a most
impressive list of Bible passages conveys to us the
absolute certainty that the removal of our guilt is
assured to us by Jesus Christ, and that "we were
reconciled to God by the death of his Son" (Romans 5.10 RSV).

*My Father and Creator, you have warned me through
the mouth of your prophet Jeremiah, "Behold, I will
bring you to judgment for saying, 'I have not sinned.' "
I won't say that Lord. I won't say anything except that I
know that your Son has reconciled me to yourself
through his death. Amen.*

HAS PRIDE MADE ME BLIND?
Job 22.1-30

God brings down the proud and saves the humble
(22.29).

The next speech by Eliphaz is designated as the beginning of the third dialogue, but genuine dialogue is no longer possible. Eliphaz is interested only in putting Job into the position of being a haughty rebel before God. "Yes," he concludes, "you must humbly return to God, and put an end to all the evil that is done in your house" (22.23).

As we hear Eliphaz speaking in this manner we cannot help but ask, "But just who is being humble and who is being proud?" We can ask this question within the church of today as we see people in opposition to one another who are not really listening to the other *person* but are merely looking for certain *words* which they can twist and attack. They want the *other* person, to be humbled, not themselves!

This human frailty led Peter, quoting from Job 22, to exhort the people of his time, "Clothe yourselves, all of you, with humility toward one another, for 'God opposes the proud, but gives grace to the humble.' Humble yourselves therefore under the mighty hand of God, that in due time he may exalt you" (1 Peter 5.5b-6 RSV).

Whose problem are we talking about, Lord? Is it not
mine? Remind me of my humble need for your grace in
Christ. Amen.

DOES GOD SEEM TO BE HIDING?
Job 23.1-17

How I wish I knew where to find him, and knew how to go where he is (23.3).

Do you feel that God is hiding? Some people might reply, "How dare you suggest such a thing! Can you not see him in all the wonders of creation?" Yet Isaiah once said, "Truly thou art a God who hidest thyself" (Isaiah 45.15a RSV). Martin Luther also said that the God we see in nature is still behind a mask. Job would have understood such thoughts. In the midst of his sufferings he openly declares to Eliphaz, "Almighty God has destroyed my courage. It is God, not the darkness, that makes me afraid . . . " (23.16-17).

How do we find God? The Greek philosophers teach that man can find God through reason. Eastern mystics say that you can find him through certain disciplines. The Bible insists that it is God who takes the initiative in revealing himself; and that when he does, it is not through an idea but through a person. God takes off his mask, and we see him at last in his Son who endures the worst kind of suffering and death which can come to man.

No matter what our trials may be, we know through Christ Jesus that God is not hiding. His love, revealed on the cross, lightens our every darkness.

Not in the stars nor the trees, but in the face of your Son, I find new faith and hope, dear God. Amen.

WHERE IS JUSTICE?
Job 24.1-25

Why doesn't God set . . . a day of justice for those who serve him? (24.1).

Job moves from point to point in expressing his bewilderment about the ways of God. He graphically describes the scandals, the exploitation, and terror in the streets which also upset us today (24.1-17). What, he asks, has happened to justice?

The thoughts in Job 24.18-25 are not those of Job but of one of his adversaries. Are they representative of our outlook as well? Do we refuse to face up to the exploitation and terror that really have a death grip on this world, perhaps dismissing these facts with pious remarks about how evil men will one day be repaid?

In the name of God, of what flesh-and-blood comfort are such words to the innocent who are being oppressed every day? We are no better, and perhaps worse, than Job's comforters if we make big generalizations about how justice will be done but then do nothing ourselves to make that justice operative.

Almighty God, help me to do more than lament over the world's sinfulness. Give me a clear vision of the needs of the oppressed and then the will to respond to those needs. Amen.

TAKE A NEW LOOK AT YOURSELF
Job 25.1-6

Then what about man, that worm, that insect? What is man worth in God's eyes? (25.6).

There are people today who are very expert in creating in themselves, or in others, what psychologists call "I'm-not-okay" feelings. These people use the Bible's teaching about the terrible sinfulness of all mankind as their point of departure.

Bildad would have felt very much at home among such people. When he last spoke, he sought to strike terror into the heart of Job. This time he seeks to create self-contempt. He calls upon Job to think of himself as nothing but an insect, a worm, someone who is worth nothing in the sight of God.

The gospel calls us to become more than mere Bildads or Zophars in our estimation of our real worth. The gospel invites us to see and believe that our worth has been determined by the value God himself has placed upon us. We were worth the sacrifice of his Son. Because of his Son's death on our behalf each of us has been made into a new person by faith. Think of it! In Christ God has declared us to be "a temple of the Holy Spirit" (1 Corinthians 6.19 RSV).

O God, you have made all things new in Christ. Through my faith in him as my Savior, give me a new estimation of myself. Amen.

THE WAY OF ALMIGHTY GOD
Job 26.1-14

When he threatens the pillars that hold up the sky, they shake and tremble with fear (26.11).

The "comforters" of Job have hammered away unceasingly on the theme that he should bow down before the almighty Creator who, they insist, even-handedly doles out both punishments and rewards exactly as they are deserved.

What about this? If we are prospering, should we think that we have been better than someone else? What about all those who prosper but are not servants of the Lord? For what are they being rewarded? And what about the many faithful who have never seen more than a few dollars at a time? What happens to all this talk about rewards if one day a man's lawyer calls up to tell him that his firm will be forced to declare bankruptcy in the morning because of a terribly miscalculated bid on its latest project?

We ought to take to heart once and for all Job's contention that God cannot be understood in such over-simplified terms. If we would understand God, then let us look to the cross. There we are reminded that our relationship with God is not determined by means of an awards system but through his grace alone.

O Heavenly Father, it is the wideness of your mercy which gives me strength to stand in the day of testing. Amen.

ARE OUR EARS CLOSED?
Job 27.1-23

I will never say that you men are right (27.5a).

At this stage in the exchanges between Job and Zophar we could well be reminded of two boxers as they face one another in about the ninth round of their bout. They stand in the middle of the ring, neither giving an inch. They keep punching away, but the sharpness is gone. They have punched themselves out.

New elements of thought are about to be injected into the Book of Job, and we probably feel that it is just as well. We have heard the same old accusations and denials many times over. However, before we move on, let us not neglect a great lesson which we can learn from witnessing these repeated exchanges. By far the most common result of bombarding a person with accusations is that spirit of self-justification which led Job to say, "I will never give up my claim to be right; my conscience is clear" (27.6).

Are there situations where we have been caught up in such a spirit? Perhaps people have been attacking us to an unwarranted degree. Nevertheless, what ought we to hear? What faults ought to be confessed so that the word of God's forgiveness might be spoken to us?

Open my ears and mind to things I need to hear. Amen.

A HYMN TO WISDOM
Job 28.1-28

God alone knows . . . the place where wisdom is found
(28.23).

The development of new techniques has launched a new wave of efforts to recover sunken treasures lying at the bottom of the Atlantic. But the search for hidden treasure is nothing new. Witness the description in Job 28 of miners who, though living thousands of years ago, showed great skill and courage as they groped their way in the darkness, clung to ropes as they dropped down into deep pits, and even dug away mountains at their base in an effort to find precious gems.

There is, however, something more elusive and of more value than "coral, or crystal, or rubies" (28.18). The highest prize of all is true wisdom. This wisdom does not come through man's cleverness. It is a gift from God and through God.

Men have always talked about finding "the key which will unlock the universe." God provides us with his own answer: "To be wise, you must fear the Lord. To understand, you must turn from evil" (28.28).

Heavenly Father, I thank you for whatever gifts of
intelligence, cleverness, or education you have given to
me; but above all, give me that wisdom which begins
with my adoration of your righteousness and holiness.
Amen.

LOOK TO THE FUTURE, NOT TO THE PAST
Job 29.1—30.31

My dignity is gone like a puff of wind (30.15b).

Job has come to the point in his life where he must say that families he would not have trusted to watch his sheep "make fun of me now!...I am nothing but a joke to them" (30.1,9b). Everything he has treasured seems gone for good: his previous closeness to God (29.2-5, cf. 30.20.), his happy family (29.5-6), the respect he once enjoyed (29.7-8), the role of a benefactor to the poor (29.9-17), and the good times when his words "sank in like drops of rain; everyone listened eagerly, the way farmers welcome the spring rains" (29.22b-23).

Who has not known Job's feeling that everything good lies in a past but better day? However, while the bittersweet memory of past glory may bring momentary satisfaction, we will get lasting strength only from the hope God offers to us. Forgetting the past, we look to the future which has already begun through the resurrection of Jesus Christ. By faith we are God's children who will share in our Lord's future, and we say confidently, "I consider that the sufferings of this present time are not worth comparing with the glory that is to be revealed to us" (Romans 8.18 RSV).

The wells of the past are dry, O Lord. You alone are my undepleted resource for the future. Amen.

A CLEAN HEART AND MIND
Job 31.1-11

God knows everything I do; he sees every step I take (31.4).

The Spirit of God now leads us into one of the Bible's greatest chapters dealing with the morality of a child of God. It begins with reflections on God-pleasing sexual behavior.

Job knows that lust is wrong. He warns the man hidden outside his neighbor's door that God sees every step he takes—and every bed that he sleeps in! He condemns adultery, describing it as a "destructive, hellish fire" which can destroy everything a man holds dear.

Dare we think that we can disarm lust or change the meaning of adultery by making jokes about them? In the age of the patriarchs Joseph said to a woman seeking to seduce him, "How then can I do this great wickedness, and sin against God?" (Genesis 39.9b RSV). Why? He knew that he belonged to God. It was this sense of having been made through Christ into the new creation of God which led the Apostle Paul to say, "But fornication and all impurity or covetousness must not even be named among you, as is fitting among saints" (Ephesians 5.3 RSV).

O God, you see both my inner self and my outward acts. I am proud of neither. But now your Son has brought me under new ownership, and I pray for the strength to live accordingly. Amen.

THE MORAL MAN CARES ABOUT HIS BROTHER
Job 31.13-23

When one of my servants complained against me, I would listen and treat him fairly. If I did not, how could I then face God? (31.13-14a).

On the surface of this chapter we hear Job replying to the various charges which have been raised against him. For instance, Eliphaz has accused Job of taking the clothes off the backs of his debtors and of abusing the poor and the fatherless (22.5,6,9). But in defending himself Job goes far beyond mere denials. He gives us one of the Bible's most magnificent expositions of what the prophets considered to be truly righteous behavior.

By the prophets' standards, the moral man is much more than one who is circumspect in matters of sex and drink. He is, as Job makes clear, a man who cares about the poor, the widows, the orphans, the hungry, and the rights of all his brothers. Morality is more than obeying the law. It is caring about the weak; it is doing something for them.

Although Christianity encourages us to think about being moral men and women, it does not direct us to become chained and uptight. Instead, through the picture of him who freely gave his life for us, we are given a freedom which expresses itself in love towards all men.

Keep me from a private piety, O Lord. Lead me to respond to the needs of your world. Amen.

GOLD AND GOD
Job 31.24-32

I have never trusted in riches (31.24).

Job replies to Eliphaz's insinuations (22.6-26) that Job has made gold his god. He denies it. It is very easy to identify with Job and say that our record is also clean. I have trouble in seeing wealth as a threat to my faith. In fact, while a search of devotional writings reveals countless pages devoted to preventing people who have suffered economic disaster from falling away from their faith, it is next to impossible to find anything which has been written with an eye to helping a believer handle a financial windfall. We all assume that this will be no problem at all!

Why, then, did Jesus say, "Do not lay up for yourselves treasures on earth, where moth and rust consume . . . . It is easier for a camel to go through the eye of a needle than for a rich man to enter the kingdom of God"? He must know something about us!

There is a saying that every man has his price. For Judas it was thirty pieces of silver. As we look soberly at our own badly twisted set of values, let us also joyously reaffirm the apostolic message that we have been bought with a great price—the life blood of Jesus (1 Corinthians 6.20; 1 Peter 1.18-19). Because of this great transaction, let us tell Jesus that he has become the silver, gold, treasury notes, and blue chip stocks of our lives.

O Jesus, you are our priceless treasure! Amen.

THE MISSING MIRROR
Job 31.33-40

Will no one listen to what I am saying? I swear that every word is true (31.35a).

In a gathering of friends from many sections of the nation I found occasion to joke with a former classmate about how he was "showing his years." As I expected, another friend laughingly asked if *I* had looked into a mirror lately!

The truth is that while all of us use a mirror, we usually do not look at the image too closely. It would tell us too much! One has the feeling that this is Job's problem. He has just given a splendid exposition of the law of God, but he is not using that law as a mirror for himself. Or at least he is not looking too closely. He defies the world and God, saying that he will gladly permit any charges against him to be placed before God and yet "hold my head high in his presence" (31.37b).

What about our use of the law? Do we chiefly use it as a spyglass to see more clearly the faults of others? Let us instead use it as a looking glass by which we see ourselves as God sees us. When we do, we may then lay aside that mirror and listen to the good news that our fellowship with God does not depend on our perfection. It is there because God has loved us, accepted us, and shown his mercy through his Son.

Thank you God, for enabling me to take a new look at myself, seeing both my faults and my Savior. Amen.

THE SPIRIT'S GIFT OF WISDOM
Job 32.1-22

It is the spirit of Almighty God that comes to men and gives them wisdom (32.8).

One day a visitor stood on the coast of England and looked out over a vast stretch of mud in which ships tilted at crazy angles. He wondered what could be done. The heaving of an anchor or the hoisting of a sail would mean nothing. It was impossible to haul in water enough to fill the basin. Then, as he watched, the tide swept in. As the waters splashed against their sides, the ships came to life again.

Who has not felt left "high and dry" with a crazy jumble of facts which simply can't be put into a sensible pattern? We often need that wisdom which we know will never come through the debates of men. How will it come? If we have been picturing Job and his three friends standing on a sort of stage, then this is the moment when a new character comes bounding down the aisle and leaps upon the stage. His name is Elihu. He is young. He is angry. He tells them, "It is the spirit of Almighty God that comes to men and gives them wisdom. It is not growing old that makes men wise, or helps them know what is right" (32.8-9).

How shall we understand the injustices and suffering of the world? It is only through our reaching out for the Spirit of God that we will be able to rest steady and upright on the sea of life.

Lord, send your Holy Spirit that he may rule and direct us according to your will and lead us into all truth. Amen.

SHARPEN MY PERCEPTION, LORD
Job 33.1-33

God speaks in many ways (33.14a).

If God would write daily messages in the sky, would we remember to look up? The Bible insists that God is always speaking. The real problem revolves around whether we are truly ready to listen.

If Elihu were to come to us as he did to Job, he would begin with words of peace: "You and I . . . are the same in God's sight, both of us were formed from clay. So you have no reason to fear me; I will not overpower you" (33.6-7). He would then point out that God speaks through dreams and visions, the chastisement of illness, angels who remind us of our duty, and divine rescue from distress (33.15,16,23,29). He would say that man, not God, is the problem: "Even though God speaks in many ways, no one pays attention to what he says" (33.14).

For us, the promise of God's revelation goes beyond Elihu's list. The writer to the Hebrews tells us the good news that "In many and various ways God spoke of old to our fathers by the prophets; but in these last days he has spoken to us by a Son" (Hebrews 1.1-2a RSV).

The Son of God is more than a set of answers. He is the living promise of God that we will be rescued from our every trouble and once again see the light of life.

Speak, O Lord. My faith gains new strength as I pause to listen to you through the voice of your Son. Amen.

SHOW ME YOUR RIGHTEOUSNESS, GOD
Job 34.1-37

Will Almighty God do what is wrong? (34.10b).

If there is someone among us who wonders how God is exercising his power; someone who asks if the suffering and injustice in the world proves that there is no rhyme or reason to the universe; someone who has concluded that God is not interested in making things right, then let him be directed by Job's own search for answers. Of course, Job's friend, Elihu, is shocked that Job would express such feelings and say, "It never does any good to try to follow God's will" (34.9). He asks Job, "Do you think the Almighty hates justice? Are you condemning the righteous God?" (34.17).

But what *should* Job or anyone else think who has borne an enormous burden of suffering? What do *we* think?

The author of the Book of Job is straining to see beyond the horizon to that answer about God's righteousness which lies in the New Testament. There we see God in Christ. He responds to the agonies of the sick and hungry. He defends and reaches out to the oppressed. In the final step of self-disclosure, God reveals his righteousness by making Jesus, who knew no sin, to be sin for us so that peace could be made between all sinful men and himself. God *is* at work. God *does* care for us mightily. Jesus shows that.

O God, while I cannot understand all things, the cross of your Son has shown me your righteousness and convinced me that in him the final victory shall be won. Amen.

ACCEPT MY BEWILDERMENT, LORD
Job 35.1-16

When men are oppressed they groan; they cry for someone to save them. But they don't turn to God, their Creator, who gives them strength in their darkest hours (35.9-10).

Is this where Job and the rest of us go wrong? Do we refuse to let our trouble lead us back to God? There are reasons why so many find it hard to turn around. They refuse to acknowledge that man's sin has caused the havoc which engulfs the world. They blame God whom they picture as one who is distant and indifferent. Even Elihu says of God: "Look at the sky! See how high the clouds are! If you sin, that does no harm to God" (35.5-6a).

But contrary to Elihu's remark, the sin of the world *has* hurt God. If righteousness, even as we see it in the world, has suffered many reverses, so was the very Son of God subjected to great suffering. In that suffering of Christ God came among us, sharing our sorrows, enduring our hurt, receiving to himself the consequences of sin.

No, we cannot understand all the reasons for suffering as we see it; but neither can we understand how God could be willing to take our suffering upon himself. But he has!

I am bewildered by many things, Lord, but nothing is more amazing than your love. In it I find my strength. Amen.

USE MY TEARS, LORD
Job 36.1-21

But God teaches men through suffering and uses distress to open their eyes (36.15).

It's not easy to smile through your tears, is it? Yet the Lord wants us to go beyond even this effort. He invites us to use those tears, which would otherwise serve only to blur our vision, in a positive manner. He would have us use them as a new set of lenses which enable us to focus even more clearly upon his purposes for our lives. Therefore Elihu pleads with Job, "Be careful not to turn to evil; your suffering was sent to keep you from it" (36.21).

No one asks for trouble. We ask for blessings. However, when trouble comes, it can be accepted as an anvil on which our pride is broken as we ask ourselves, "What is God saying to me that I have been ignoring? What new strength does the Lord want me to discover?" Then trouble becomes the means to a blessing, and we understand the Word: "Count it all joy, my brethren, when you meet various trials, for you know that the testing of your faith produces steadfastness" (James 1.2-3 RSV).

When we believe that God's loving presence can be found in the midst of our troubles, we do more than endure. We overcome.

Heavenly Father, I cannot understand everything that is happening. But I trust in your unchanging love. I believe that the day will come when we will at last see the value of every tear shed here on earth. Amen.

STILL MY TONGUE, O LORD
Job 36.22—37.24

Pause a moment and . . . consider the wonderful things God does (37.14).

The words of Elihu ought to be read aloud and then read again as the glory of God is lifted up before our eyes. God takes up water from the earth and sends it back in showers (36.27-28). He sends clouds scudding across the sky while the thunder roars and lightning brightens the sky and strikes the earth (36.29-33). Through the force of falling snow and driving rain he brings to a halt the activities of man and beast (37.6-8). Who cares if we can give "scientific" explanations of these phenomena? Are they not still from God?

Elihu's obvious thrill in seeing the works of nature tells us much about our own irreligious age. We have insulated ourselves against the impact of God's creation. We design windows that cannot be opened. We seal ourselves in air-conditioned cars. We pave over, exterminate, and obliterate the Lord's handiwork at every turn. As a consequence, we do not see God either.

This final speech on the part of Elihu serves as a prelude to that moment when, at last, God will speak for himself. Even now, as the awesome displays of nature speak of his glory, let us be silent before him.

O Lord, let my tongue be stilled and my mind filled with wonder as I behold those signs of your glory which are all around me. Amen.

AT YOUR SERVICE, LORD
Job 38.1—39.30

Stand up now like a man (38.3a).

Job, in the manner of a prince-to-prince confrontation, wanted to contend with God as an equal. The Bible has something special to say to such human pretensions. It reminds us that the Son of God, the eternal Word by whom all the glories of nature as they are described in Job 38 and 39, "did not count equality with God a thing to be grasped, but emptied himself, taking the form of a servant, being born in the likeness of men" (Philippians 2.6b-7 RSV).

If the Son of God came among us in the spirit of service, then we ought to find our true identity in expressing our humanity just as he did. We should not, as Bildad once suggested to Job, consider ourselves as nothing but worthless worms. But neither are we heavenly princes. We have an entirely new vision of what it means to be truly human. We want to be renewed in the image of him who came among us as a servant, obedient, for our sake, even to death on a cross.

In our renewed humanity, which rises up out of faith in Christ, we can give God that kind of glory and praise which the rest of creation, for all its majesty and splendor, can never give. We can give him our hearts.

O God, help me to be nothing more and nothing less than you have fashioned me to be: your child dedicated to service even as your Son came to serve and to rescue us. Amen.

Job 40.1—41.34

Job, you challenged Almighty God (40.1).

Job has struggled with God and insisted that God owes *him* an answer. People do that. But God replies that it is time for Job to remember his human limitations. God asks if Job can make the monster Behemoth or the Leviathan. We do not need to determine to which species these beasts belong. What we do need to remember is that it is God himself who lets loose *all* the mighty forces which are displayed in this universe.

The thought that it is God who holds all things in his hands can be found throughout Scripture. "Behold, like the clay in the potter's hand, so are you in my hand, O house of Israel" (Jeremiah 18.6b RSV). "Who are you, a man, to answer back to God? Will what is molded say to its molder, 'Why have you made me thus?' " (Romans 9.20 RSV).

Something must happen to us before our proud hearts will accept such an assertion. There must be surrender. But surrender is not always the submission of a weaker person to a more powerful adversary. Surrender can also be a part of an act of love, in this case, love for God. Instead of challenging God, we can offer love's surrender as we ponder the Lord's most mysterious and majestic act of all, the loving sacrifice of his own dear Son.

Father, in the name of Jesus who loved me, I surrender my life, my spirit, my everything, into your hands. Amen.

SEEING GOD
Job 42.1-6

Now I have seen you with my own eyes (42.5b).

"Has anybody here seen God?" This would be a good question for any gathering. Many talk about God, but it is another thing to be able to say, as Job did, "Then I knew only what others had told me, but now I have seen you with my own eyes" (42.5).

What enabled Job to say this? Was he at last given a rational explanation concerning his suffering? No, he was not; and neither can we expect such an answer for everything that comes into our lives. No human being can give an intellectual answer to some of the heart's deepest questions.

What makes it possible for us to see God? In an earlier age the Lord primarily pointed to himself through his awesome works in nature. But now we can rejoice that God has revealed himself in his mightiest act of all: the death and resurrection of Jesus. He has given us a living Christ through whom every tear shall be wiped away and every enemy, including death, finally abolished.

Have we only heard of God? We can do more. Through Christ we can see him!

Open my eyes to my sin, O Lord, and lead me to repent. Open my eyes to your Son and lead me to rejoice. Amen.

PATIENCE REWARDED
James 5.7-11

You have heard of Job's patience, and you know how the Lord provided for him in the end (5.11 TEV).

A farmer plants in the spring and then waits for his labor to develop from a promise into a fully-ripened and precious fruit. A prophet sows the seed of a thought, confident, despite persecution, that time and truth will win out. This is the kind of patience James is talking about when he holds up the picture of Job before his readers.

It is altogether fitting to salute Job's patience. In so doing we are not forgetting how, in a demonstration of the feelings shared by all of us, he bitterly protested against his lot. On the other hand, patience is always more than helpless and silent resignation to one's fate. Patience is an attitude. It contains a mixture of that God-given help which provides us with the strength to contend against all obstacles and the grace to leave the final outcome in God's hands.

The Apostle Paul writes, "Whatever was written in former days was written for our instruction, that by steadfastness and by the encouragement of the scriptures we might have hope" (Romans 15.4 RSV). The church praises God for the drama of Jesus' victory over death, but we give thanks to God also for the Book of Job. We know that in the end God will provide for his own.

May the God of steadfastness and encouragement enable us to live with hope undimmed by the trials of this life. Amen.

A SACRIFICIAL PRAYER
Job 42.7-8

Now take seven bulls and seven rams to Job and offer them as a sacrifice for yourselves (42.8a).

Lord, we have witnessed Job's long struggle with his friends. If he was proud, they were harsh. If you spoke sternly to Job, neither were you pleased with the emptiness of soul displayed by Zophar, Bildad, and Eliphaz.

But this is no time to sit in judgment on others. You have led us to examine ourselves for evidence of our own stubborn resistance to your will and our own spirit of judgment against others.

Lead us to receive your Word and to partake of the Holy Supper instituted by your Son, for hearing the words, "given for you," and "shed for you," and for remembering your love, O Lord. We rejoice that now it is everlastingly true that:

> *He blotted out with his own blood*
> *The judgment that against us stood;*
> *He full atonement for us made,*
> *And all our debt he fully paid.*
> *That this is now and ever true*
> *He gives an earnest ever new:*
> *In this his holy Supper here*
> *We taste his love so sweet, so near.*
>   *Amen.*

THE NEW WAY OF FAITH
Job 42.9-11

The Lord made him prosperous again (42.10).

The question always arises: "Why did such a good man as Job suffer so greatly?" This is also the first question raised concerning Jesus' suffering.

However, the Book of Job has taken us beyond this question to that theme which is at the very heart of both the New Testament and the life of Jesus. How shall the great gap between unrighteous man and his holy Creator ever be closed?

Job found the answer. It was not in his claims about being a righteous man. As we see him begin to enjoy the blessings which earlier had marked his life, we are looking at a different man. He is finished with his former practice of justifying himself before God. Faith has become Job's way. He has accepted what once he insisted must be proved. God is God. He is good. God is righteous. He gives life and man simply receives it.

We, in the manner of Job, can come to a similar conclusion about ourselves: "Then what becomes of our boasting? It is excluded . . . . Our acquittal is not based on our good deeds; it is based on what Christ has done and our faith in him" (Romans 3.27 RSV and The Living Bible). This is God's answer to man's greatest question.

I thank you with all my heart, O God, that the cross of Jesus has bridged the gap I could never close. Amen.

GREAT DAY AHEAD
Job 42.12-17

The Lord blessed the last part of Job's life even more than ... the first (42.12a).

Chained in the depths. Waiting for the dawn. Dazzled again by the light of God's love. This is the story of God's children. It is the story of Job. Crushed and confused, desperately maintaining that "there is someone in heaven to stand up for me" (16.19; 19.25), and then finding God pouring down blessings as never before, Job stands for everyman.

As we await help for our troubles, we dare to draw this encouragement from Job's life. Whatever our depths, however foolish our hopes might seem to others, we know that the Redeemer who can rescue us lives even now. He is Jesus, the living Lord who has overcome the bonds of death. Because he lives, he is not a figure in the dim past. Jesus is in the now, standing by us in our troubles.

Because Jesus lives, we can also look beyond today. As little as we can comprehend the full extent of the agonies which fill today's world, even less can we perceive the glories of the restored creation which he will usher in. But it will happen. That day will dawn. Jesus is in the present, and he is also in our future. He is the world's future. Through him it shall be made new and perfect. As Job learned, we have that kind of God.

Yes, Lord, you give and you take away. But through the hope of the resurrection we know that that day is coming when you will restore a hundredfold. Amen.

OUR SURE HOPE
1 Corinthians 15.51-57

But thanks be to God, who gives us the victory through our Lord Jesus Christ (15.57 RSV).

"I know that my Redeemer lives!" This exultant phrase from a beloved hymn sums up not only the thoughts of Job but of every Christian. These words are our answer to a world in which the powers which exult in the creation of war, pestilence, suffering, and injustice seem to hold sway.

We know that God is still in charge of history. Few believe this today. Not many believed it when Jesus first rose from the dead and appeared to his disciples. Nevertheless, he has brought hope where there was only despair. He has made possible the "tension of faith" whereby we, while others can only weep, may joyfully sing,

> The proud with all their plans of conquest
>   shall be scattered;
> The mighty ones shall be brought low,
> The lowly lifted up, the hungry fed,
> And the rich sent empty away.
>
>   (cf. Luke 2.52-53)

Whatever we might think should be the order of human events, let us rejoice in the knowledge that God knows what he is doing. In the risen Christ he has already given us the "first-fruits" of the final victory over all the powers of darkness. This is our sure hope.

He lives! He lives! What comfort this sweet sentence gives! Amen.

JOB

for Modern Man

Today's English Version

PREFACE

THE BOOK OF JOB is one of the most widely read parts of the Bible and is regarded as one of the literary masterpieces of the world. As a part of the biblical material called "Wisdom Literature," the book deals with important questions of right and wrong, reward and punishment, happiness and misery. But because Job suffered, even though he was good and was faithful to God, this book goes beyond earlier Wisdom Literature to probe the basic questions of why the innocent suffer, and what is the relationship between man and God.

In the prose introduction, God permits Satan to test Job by destroying his family and his property and then by sending Job a painful disease. In spite of his suffering, Job refuses to blame God for what has happened to him.

The major part of the book is in poetry. In it three of Job's friends talk with him. He maintains that he is innocent, but they repeat the traditional beliefs and insist that Job's suffering is his punishment for sinning. Job does not give in and is finally able to state firmly that he trusts God even though he cannot understand what God is doing.

After a speech by a fourth friend, who also believes that Job has sinned, God himself speaks. God's description of his power and of the wonders of the world he has created leads Job to see his own weakness and to express once more his faith in God. God reprimands

PREFACE

Job's friends and makes Job even more prosperous than he was at first.

Like the New Testament in *Today's English Version,* this is a distinctively new translation that does not conform to traditional vocabulary and style, but seeks to express the meaning of the Hebrew text in words and forms accepted as standard by people everywhere who employ English as a means of communication. Because the book of Job is in the form of drama, the different speakers are identified in the margin. The poetic form of this translation does not try to follow the Hebrew rhythm, but attempts to express in natural English rhythms the emotion and the meaning of the various speeches.

Where there is general agreement that the Hebrew text cannot be translated as it now stands, the translation employs the evidence of other ancient texts or follows present-day scholarly consensus. All such modifications are identified in footnotes. Other footnotes give information designed to help the reader understand the meaning of the text, especially where ancient beliefs are expressed or alluded to.

THE BOOK OF JOB

Satan Tests Job

1 There was a man named Job, who lived in the land of Uz.*a* He worshiped God and was faithful to him. He was a good man, careful not to do anything evil. ² He had seven sons and three daughters, ³ and owned 7,000 sheep, 3,000 camels, 1,000 head of cattle, and 500 donkeys. He also had a large number of servants and was by far the richest man in the East.

⁴ His sons used to take turns giving a feast, to which all the others would come, and they always invited their three sisters to join them. ⁵ After each feast was over, Job would get up early the next morning and offer sacrifices in order to purify his children. He always did this because he thought that one of them might have sinned by insulting God unintentionally.

⁶ When the day came for the heavenly beings*b* to appear before the Lord, Satan*c* was there among them. ⁷ The Lord asked him, "What have you been doing?"

Satan answered, "I have been walking here and there, roaming around the earth."

⁸ The Lord said, "Did you notice my servant Job? There is no one on earth as faithful and good as he is. He worships me and is careful not to do anything evil."

⁹ Satan replied, "Would Job worship you if he got nothing out of it? ¹⁰ You have protected him and his family and everything he owns. You bless everything he does, and you have given him enough cattle to fill the whole country. ¹¹ But now suppose you take away everything he has—he will curse you to your face."

---

a UZ: An area whose exact location is unknown. *b* HEAVENLY BEINGS: Supernatural beings who serve God in heaven. *c* SATAN: A supernatural being whose name indicates he was regarded as man's opponent.

¹² The Lord said to Satan, "All right, everything he has is in your power, but you must not hurt Job himself." So Satan left.

Job's Children and Wealth Are Destroyed

¹³ One day when Job's children were having a feast at the home of their oldest brother, ¹⁴ a messenger came running to Job. "We were plowing the fields with the cattle," he said, "and the donkeys were in a nearby pasture. ¹⁵ Suddenly the Sabeans*d* attacked and stole them all. They killed every one of your servants except me. I am the only one who escaped to tell you."

¹⁶ Before he finished speaking, another servant came and said, "Lightning struck the sheep and the shepherds and killed them all. I am the only one who escaped to tell you."

¹⁷ Before he finished speaking, another servant came and said, "Three bands of Chaldean*e* raiders attacked us, took away the camels, and killed all your servants except me. I am the only one who escaped to tell you."

¹⁸ Before he finished speaking, another servant came and said, "Your children were having a feast at the home of your oldest son, ¹⁹ when a storm swept in from the desert. It blew the house down and killed them all. I am the only one who escaped to tell you."

²⁰ Then Job got up and tore his clothes in grief. He shaved his head and threw himself face downward on the ground. ²¹ He said, "I was born with nothing and I will die with nothing. The Lord gave, and now he has taken away. May his name be praised!" ²² In spite of everything that had happened, Job did not sin by blaming God.

Satan Tests Job Again

2 When the day came for the heavenly beings to appear before the Lord again, Satan was there among them. ² The Lord asked him, "Where have you been?"

d SABEANS: A tribe of wandering raiders from the south. *e* CHALDEANS: A tribe of wandering raiders from the north.

Satan answered, "I have been walking here and there, roaming around the earth."

³ The Lord asked, "Did you notice my servant Job? There is no one on earth as faithful and good as he is. He worships me and is careful not to do anything evil. You persuaded me to let you attack him for no reason at all, but Job is still as faithful as ever."

⁴ Satan replied, "A man will give up everything in order to stay alive. ⁵ But now suppose you hurt his body—he will curse you to your face."

⁶ So the Lord said to Satan, "All right, he is in your power, but you are not to kill him."

⁷ Then Satan left the Lord's presence and made sores break out all over Job's body. ⁸ Job went and sat by the garbage dump and took a piece of broken pottery to scrape his sores. ⁹ His wife said to him, "You are still as faithful as ever, aren't you? Why don't you curse God and die?"

¹⁰ Job answered, "You are talking nonsense! When God sends us something good we welcome it. How can we complain when he sends us trouble?" Even in all this suffering Job did not say anything against God.

Job's Friends Come

¹¹ Three of Job's friends were Eliphaz, from the city of Teman,ᶠ Bildad, from the land of Shuah,ᵍ and Zophar, from the land of Namah.ʰ When they heard how much Job had been suffering, they decided to go visit him and comfort him. ¹² While they were still a long way off they saw Job, but did not recognize him. When they did, they began to weep and wail. They tore their clothes in grief and threw dust into the air and on their heads. ¹³ Then they sat there on the ground with him for seven days and nights without saying a word, because they saw how much he was suffering.

ᶠ TEMAN: A city in the country of Edom, southeast of Palestine. ᵍ SHUAH: A region possibly near the Euphrates River, or perhaps in northern Arabia. ʰ NAMAH: A region whose exact location is unknown.

¹⁷ In the grave wicked men stop their evil,
 and tired workmen rest at last.
¹⁸ Even prisoners enjoy peace,
 free from shouts and harsh commands.
¹⁹ Everyone is there, great and small alike,
 and slaves at last are free.

²⁰ Why let men go on living in misery?
 Why give light to men in grief?
²¹ They wait for death, but it never comes;
 they prefer a grave to any treasure.
²² They are not happy till they are dead and
  buried;
²³ God keeps their future hidden
 and hems them in on every side.
²⁴ Instead of eating, I mourn,
 and I can never stop groaning;
²⁵ everything I fear and dread comes true.
²⁶ I have no peace, no rest,
 and my trouble never ends.

The First Dialogue
(4.1—14.22)

4

Eliphaz
¹⁻² Job, will you be upset if I speak?
 I can't keep quiet any longer.
³ You have taught many people
 and given strength to feeble hands.
⁴ When someone stumbled, weak and tired,
 your words encouraged him to stand.
⁵ Now your turn has come for trouble,
 and you are too stunned to face it.
⁶ You worshiped God, and your life was
  blameless;
 you should have confidence and hope.

⁷ Think back now. Name a single case
   when a righteous man met with disaster.
⁸ I have seen people plow fields of evil
   and plant wickedness like seed;
      now they harvest wickedness and evil.
⁹ In his anger, God destroys them like a
   storm.
¹⁰ The wicked roar and growl like lions,
   but God silences them and breaks their
   teeth.
¹¹ Like lions with nothing to kill and eat,
   they die and their children are all scat-
   tered.

¹² Once a message came quietly,
   so quietly I could hardly hear it.
¹³ It was like a nightmare which disturbed
   my sleep.
¹⁴   I trembled and shuddered;
   my whole body shook with fear.
¹⁵ A light breeze touched my face,
   and my skin crawled with fright.
¹⁶ I could see something standing there;
   I stared, but couldn't tell what it was.
   Then I heard a voice out of the silence,
¹⁷ "Can a man be right in the sight of God?
   Can anyone be pure before his Creator?
¹⁸ God does not trust his heavenly servants;ᵏ
   he finds fault with his angels.
¹⁹ Do you think he will trust a creature of
   clay,
      a thing of dust that can be crushed like
      a moth?
²⁰ A man may be alive in the morning,
   but die unnoticed before evening comes.
²¹ All that he has is taken away;
   he dies, still lacking wisdom."

ᵏ HEAVENLY SERVANTS: Supernatural beings who served God in heaven;
also called "messengers," or "angels."

5   Call out, Job. See if anyone answers.
    Is there any angel to whom you can
      turn?
2 To worry yourself to death with resent-
    ment
      would be a foolish, senseless thing to
      do.
3 I have seen fools who looked secure,
    but I called down a sudden curse on
      their homes.
4 Their sons can never find safety;
    in court no one stands up to defend
      them.
5 Hungry people will eat the fool's crops—
    even the grain growing among thorns—
    and thirsty people will envy his wealth.
6 Evil does not grow in the soil,
    nor does trouble grow out of the ground.
7 No! Man brings trouble on himself,
    as surely as sparks fly up from a fire.

8 If I were you, I would turn to God
    and present my case to him.
9 We cannot understand the great things he
    does,
    and there is no end to his miracles.
10 He sends rain on the land and waters the
    fields.
11 Yes, it is God who raises the humble
    and gives joy to all who mourn.
12-13 He upsets the plans of tricky men,
    and traps wise men in their own
      schemes,
    so that nothing they do succeeds;
14   even at noon they grope in darkness.
15 But God saves the poor[l] from death;
    he saves the needy from oppression.
16 He gives hope to the poor and silences the
    wicked.

l poor; *Hebrew unclear.*

¹⁷ Happy is the person whom God corrects!
    Do not resent it when he reprimands
    you.
¹⁸ God bandages the wounds he makes;
    his hand hurts you, and his hand heals.
¹⁹ Time after time he will keep you from
    harm;
²⁰   when famine comes, he will keep you
    alive,
    and in war protect you from death.
²¹ God rescues you from lies and slander;
    he saves you when destruction comes.
²² You will laugh at violence and hunger
    and not be afraid of wild animals.
²³ The fields you plow will be free of rocks;
    wild animals will never attack you.
²⁴ Then you will live at peace in your tent;
    when you look at your sheep, you will
    find them safe.
²⁵ You will have as many children
    as there are blades of grass in a pasture.
²⁶ Like wheat that ripens till harvest time,
    you will live to a ripe old age.
²⁷ Job, we have learned this by long study.
    It is true, so now accept it.

6

Job

¹⁻² If my troubles and griefs were weighed on
    scales,
³   they would weigh more than the sands
    of the sea.
My wild words should not surprise you—
⁴   Almighty God has shot me with arrows,
    and their poison spreads through my
    body.
God has lined up his terrors against me.

⁵ A donkey is content when eating grass,
   and a cow is quiet when eating hay.
⁶ But who can eat flat, unsalted food?
   What taste is there in the white of an
      egg?
⁷ I have no appetite for food like that,
   and everything I eat makes me sick.ᵐ

ᵐ sick; *Hebrew unclear.*

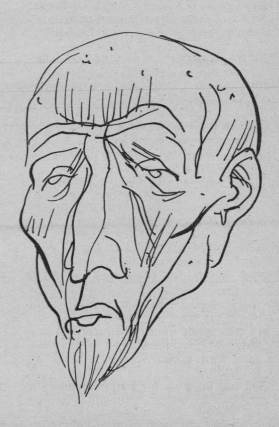

⁸ Why won't God give me what I ask?
  Why won't he answer my prayer?
⁹ I wish he would go ahead and kill me,
¹⁰ If I knew he would, I would leap for joy,
  no matter how great my pain.
  I know that God is holy;
    I have never opposed what he com-
    mands.
¹¹ What strength do I have to keep on living?
  Why go on living when I have no hope?
¹² Am I made of stone? Is my body bronze?
¹³ I have no strength left to save myself;
  there is nowhere I can turn for help.

¹⁴ In trouble[n] like this I need loyal friends—
  whether I've forsaken God or not.
¹⁵ But you, my friends, you deceive me like
    a stream
  that goes dry when no rain comes.
¹⁶⁻¹⁷ The stream is full of snow and ice,
  but in the heat they disappear,
  and the stream bed lies bare and dry.
¹⁸ Caravans get lost looking for water;
  they wander and die in the desert.
¹⁹ Caravans from Sheba and Tema[o] search,
²⁰   but their hope dies beside dry streams.
²¹ You are like those streams to me;
  you see my fate and are shocked.
²² Have I asked you to give me a gift,
  or to bribe someone on my behalf,
²³   or to save me from some enemy or ty-
    rant?

²⁴ All right, teach me; tell me my faults.
  I will be quiet and listen to you.
²⁵ An intelligent argument might convince
    me,
  but you are talking nonsense.
²⁶ You think I am talking nothing but wind;
  then why do you answer my words of
    despair?

n trouble; *Hebrew unclear.* o SHEBA AND TEMA: Towns in Arabia which
were centers of commerce.

27 You would even roll dice for orphan
    slaves,
    and make yourselves rich off your clos-
    est friends!
28 Look me in the face. I won't lie.
29 You have gone far enough. Stop being
    unjust.
    Don't condemn me. I'm in the right.
30 But still you think I am lying—
    you think I can't tell right from wrong.

7   Human life is like forced army service,
        like a life of hard manual labor,
2   like a slave longing for cool shade;
    like a worker waiting for his pay.
3 Month after month I have nothing to live
    for;
    night after night brings me grief.
4 When I lie down to sleep, the hours drag;
    I toss all night and long for dawn.
5 My body is full of worms;
    it is covered with scabs;
    pus runs out of my sores.
6 My days have passed without hope,
    passed faster than a weaver's shuttle.*

7 Remember, God, my life is only wind;
    my happiness has already ended.
8 You see me now, but never again.
    If you look for me, I'll be gone.
9-10 Like a cloud that fades and is gone,
    a man dies and never returns;
    he is forgotten by all who knew him.
11 No! I can't be quiet!
    I am angry and bitter.
    I have to speak.

---

*WEAVER'S SHUTTLE: A small device in the loom which carries threads back and forth rapidly in weaving cloth.

12 Why do you keep me under guard?
Do you think I am a sea monster?[q]
13 I lie down and try to rest;
I look for some help for my pain.
14 But you—you terrify me with dreams;
you send me visions and nightmares,
15 until I would rather be strangled,
rather die than live like this.
16 I give up. I am tired of living.
Leave me alone. My life makes no sense.

17 Why is man so important to you?
Why pay attention to what he does?
18 You inspect him every morning and test him every minute.
19 Won't you look away long enough
for me to swallow my spit?
20 Are you harmed by my sin, you jailer?
Why use me for your target practice?
Am I that big a burden to you?
21 Can't you ever forgive my sin?
Can't you pardon the wrong I do?
Soon I will lie down in the dust,
and I'll be gone when you look for me.

8

Bildad

1-2 Are you finally through with your windy speech?
3 God never twists justice;
he never fails to do what is right.
4 Your children must have sinned against God,
and so he punished them the way they deserved.

[q] SEA MONSTER: This is a reference to ancient stories in which sea monsters had to be guarded so that they would not escape and do damage.

5 But now turn and plead with Almighty
    God;
6   if you are so pure and honest,
    then God will come and help you
    and restore your household as your re-
        ward.
7 All the wealth you lost will be nothing
    compared to what God will give you
        then.

8 Look for a moment at ancient wisdom;
    consider the truths our fathers learned.
9 Our life is so short we know nothing at all;
    we are only shadows on the face of the
        earth.
10 But let the ancient wise men teach you;
    listen to what they had to say:

¹¹ "Reeds can't grow where there is no water;
     they are never found outside a swamp.
¹² If the water dries up they are the first to
          wither,
     while still too small to be cut and used.
¹³ Godless men are like those reeds;
     their hope is gone, once God is for-
          gotten.
¹⁴ They trust a thread—a spider web.
¹⁵   If they lean on a web, will it hold them
          up?
     If they grab for a thread, will it help
          them stand?"

¹⁶ Evil men sprout like weeds in the sun,
     like weeds that spread all through the
          garden.
¹⁷ Their roots wrap around the stones
     and hold fast to[r] every rock.
¹⁸ But then pull them up—
     no one will ever know they were there.
¹⁹ Yes, that's all the joy evil men have;
     others now come and take their places.

²⁰ But God will never abandon the faithful,
     or ever give help to evil men.
²¹ He will let you laugh and shout again,
²²   but he will bring disgrace on those who
          hate you,
     and the homes of the wicked will dis-
          appear.

[r] hold fast to; *Hebrew* sees.

9

Job

¹⁻² Yes, I've heard all that before.
   But how can a man win his case against
      God?
³ How can anyone argue with him?
   He can ask a thousand questions
      that no one could ever answer.
⁴ God is so wise and powerful
   no man can stand up against him.
⁵ Without warning he moves mountains
   and destroys them in anger.
⁶ God sends earthquakes and shakes the
      ground;
   he rocks the pillars^s the earth stands on.
⁷ God can keep the sun from rising,
   and the stars from shining at night.
⁸ No one helped God stretch out the heav-
      ens
   or trample the sea monster's back.^{t}
⁹ God hung the stars in the sky—the Dip-
      per,^{u}
      Orion,^{v} the Pleiades,^{w} and the stars of
         the south.^{x}
¹⁰ We cannot understand the great things he
      does,
   and there is no end to his miracles.

¹¹ God passes by, but I cannot see him.
¹² He takes what he wants, and no one can
      stop him;
      no one can ask him, "What are you
         doing?"

---

^{s} PILLARS: In ancient times, people believed the earth was held up by
pillars (see also 26.11). ^{t} TRAMPLE THE SEA MONSTER'S BACK: This is
a reference to ancient stories in which a sea monster was killed and
then trampled (see also 26.13). ^{u} THE DIPPER: A group of stars resembling a water dipper, also known as *Ursa Major*, "Great Bear."
^{v} ORION: A group of stars named for the great hunter Orion.
^{w} PLEIADES: A group of stars named for the seven daughters of the
ancient hero Atlas. ^{x} STARS OF THE SOUTH: A group of stars that
cannot now be identified.

¹³ God's anger is constant. He crushed his
enemies
    who helped Rahab,^y the sea monster,
    oppose him.
¹⁴ So how can I find words to answer God?
¹⁵ Though I am innocent, all I can do
    is beg for mercy from God my judge.
¹⁶ Yet even then, if he lets me speak,
    I can't believe he would listen to me.
¹⁷ He sends storms to batter and bruise me,
    without any reason at all.
¹⁸ He won't let me get my breath;
    all he has done to me makes me bitter.
¹⁹ Should I try force? Try force on God?
  Should I take him to court? Who would
    make him go?
²⁰ I am innocent and faithful, but my words
    sound guilty,
    and everything I say seems to condemn
    me.
²¹⁻²² I am innocent, but I no longer care.
    I am sick of living. Nothing matters;
    innocent or guilty, God will destroy us.
²³ When an innocent man suddenly dies,
    God laughs.
²⁴ God gave the world to the wicked.
  He made all the judges blind.
  And if God didn't do it, who did?

²⁵ My days race by, not one of them good.
²⁶ My life passes like the swiftest boat,
    as fast as an eagle swooping down on a
    rabbit.
²⁷⁻²⁸ If I smile and try to forget my pain,
    all my suffering comes back to haunt
    me;
    I know that God holds me guilty.
²⁹ Since God holds me guilty, why should I
    bother?
³⁰   No soap can wash away my sins.

---

^y RAHAB: An imaginary sea monster, thought to be like a huge lizard
(see also 26.12 and Ps. 89.10).

31 God throws me into a pit of filth,
    and even my clothes are ashamed of
      me.
32 If God were human I could answer him
    back;
    we could go to court to decide our
      quarrel.
33 But there is no one to step between us—
    no one to judge both God and me.
34 Stop punishing me, God! Keep your ter-
    rors away!
35 I am not afraid. I am going to talk,
    because I know my own heart.

10   I am tired of living.
    Listen to how bitter I am.
2 Don't condemn me, God.
    Tell me what the charge against me is.
3 Is it right for you to be so cruel?
    To despise what you yourself have
      made?
    And then to smile on the schemes of
      wicked men?
4 Do you see things as men do?
5   Is your life as short as ours?
6 Then why do you track down all my sins
    and hunt down every fault I have?
7 You know that I am not guilty,
    that no one can save me from you.

8 Your hands formed and shaped me,
    and now[z] those same hands destroy me.
9 Remember that you made me from clay;
    are you going to crush me back to dust?
10 You gave my father strength to beget me;
    you made me grow in my mother's
      womb.
11 You framed my body with bones and
    sinews
    and covered the bones with muscles
      and skin.

z *Some ancient translations* and now; *Hebrew* together.

¹² You have given me life and constant love,
    and your care has kept me alive.
¹³ But now I know that all that time
    you had a secret purpose for me.
¹⁴ You were watching to see if I would sin,
    so you could refuse to forgive me.
¹⁵ As soon as I sin, I'm in trouble with you,
    but when I do right, I get no credit.
    I am miserable and covered with shame.
¹⁶ If I have any success at all,
    you hunt me down like a lion;
    you even work miracles to hurt me.
¹⁷ You always have some witness against me;
    your anger toward me grows and grows;
    you always have some new attack.

¹⁸ Why, God, did you let me be born?
    I should have died before anyone saw
    me.
¹⁹ To go from the womb straight to the grave
    would have been as good as never exist-
    ing.
²⁰ Isn't my life almost over? Leave me alone!
    Let me enjoy the time I have left.
²¹ I am going soon and will never come back—
    going to a dark, gloomy land,*
²²   a land of darkness, shadows, and con-
    fusion,
    where even the light is darkness.

11

Zophar

¹⁻² Will no one answer all this nonsense?
    Does talking so much put a man in the
    right?
³ Job, do you think we can't answer you?
    That your mocking words will leave us
    speechless?

a A DARK, GLOOMY LAND: It was thought that the dead continued to exist in a dark world under the ground.

⁴ You claim what you say is true;
    you claim you are pure in God's sight.
⁵ How I wish God would answer you back!
⁶ He would tell you there are many sides to
    wisdom;
    there are things too deep for human
    knowledge.
    God is punishing you less than you de-
    serve.

⁷ Can you discover the limits and bounds
    of the greatness and power of God?
⁸ The sky is no limit to God,
    but it lies beyond your reach.
    God knows the world of the dead,ᵇ
    but you do not know it.
⁹ God's greatness is broader than the earth,
    wider than the sea.
¹⁰ If God arrests you and brings you to trial,
    who is there to stop him?
¹¹ God knows which men are worthless;
    he sees all their evil deeds.
¹² Stupid men will start being wise
    when wild donkeys are born tame.

ᵇ WORLD OF THE DEAD: See 10.21.

¹³ Put your heart right, Job. Reach out to God.

¹⁴ Put away evil and wrong from your home.

¹⁵ Then face the world again, firm and courageous.

¹⁶ Then all your troubles will fade from your memory,

  like floods that are past and remembered no more.

¹⁷ Your life will be brighter than sunshine at noon,

  and life's darkest hours will shine like the dawn.

¹⁸ You will live secure and full of hope;

  God will protect you and give you rest.

¹⁹ You won't be afraid of any enemy;

  many people will ask you for help.

²⁰ But the wicked will look around in despair,

  and find that there is no way to escape.

Their only hope is that death will come.

12

Job

¹⁻² Yes, you are the voice of the people.

  When you die, wisdom will die with you.

³ But I have as much sense as you have;

  I am in no way inferior to you;

   everyone knows all that you have said.

⁴ Even my friends laugh at me now,

  they laugh, although I am righteous and blameless;

   but there was a time when God answered my prayers.

⁵ You have no troubles, and yet you make fun of me;

  you hit a man who is about to fall.

⁶ But thieves and godless men live in peace,

  though their only god is their own strength.

7 Even birds and animals have a lot they
      could teach you;
8   ask the creatures of earth and sea for
      their wisdom.
9 All of them know that the Lord's hand
      made them.
10 It is God who directs the lives of his crea-
      tures;
      every man's life is in his power.
11 But just as your tongue enjoys tasting food,
      your ears enjoy listening to words.

12-13 Old men have wisdom,
      but God has wisdom and power.
      Old men have insight;
      God has insight and power to act.
14 When God tears down, who can rebuild,
      and who can free the man God impris-
      ons?
15 Drought comes when God withholds rain;
      floods come when he turns water loose.

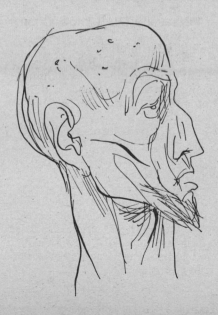

¹⁶ God is strong and always victorious,
    both cheater and cheated are under
        God's control.
¹⁷ He destroys the wisdom of rulers,
    and makes leaders act like fools.
¹⁸ He dethrones kings and makes them pris-
        oners;
¹⁹   he humbles priests and men of power.
²⁰ He silences men who are trusted,
    and takes the wisdom of old men away.
²¹ He disgraces those in power,
    and puts an end to the strength of rulers.
²² He sends light to places dark as death.
²³ He makes nations strong and great,
    but then he defeats and destroys them.
²⁴ He makes their leaders foolish,
    and lets them wander, confused and lost;
²⁵   they grope in the dark and stagger like
        drunkards.

13 ¹⁻² Everything you say, I have heard
        before.
    I understand it all. I know as much as
        you do.
    I'm not your inferior.
³ But my dispute is with God, not you;
    I want to argue my case with him.
⁴ You cover up your ignorance with lies;
    you are like doctors who can't heal any-
        one.
⁵ Say nothing, and someone may think you
        are wise!

⁶ Listen to me state my case.
⁷   Why are you lying?
    Do you think your lies will help God?
⁸ Are you trying to defend God?
    Are you going to argue his case in
        court?
⁹ If God looks at you closely will he find
        anything good?

Do you think you can fool God, the
way you fool men?
¹⁰ Even though your prejudice is hidden,
he will reprimand you,
¹¹   and his power will fill you with terror.
¹² How stale your proverbs and arguments
are!
¹³ Be quiet and give me a chance to speak,
and let the results be what they will.

¹⁴ I am*c* ready to risk my life.
¹⁵ I've lost all hope, so what if God kills me?
I am going to state my case to him.
¹⁶ It may even be that my boldness will save
me,
since no wicked man would dare face
God.
¹⁷ Now listen to my words of explanation.
¹⁸ I am ready to state my case,
because I know I am in the right.

¹⁹ God, are you going to come and accuse
me?
If you do, I am ready to be silent and
die.
²⁰ Let me ask for two things; agree to them,
and I will not try to hide from you:
²¹   stop punishing me, and don't crush me
with terror.

²² Speak first, God, and I will answer.
Or let me speak and you answer me.
²³ Of how many wrongs and sins am I guilty?
What crimes am I charged with?

²⁴ Why do you avoid me?
Why do you treat me like an enemy?
²⁵ Are you trying to frighten me? I'm nothing
but a leaf;
you are attacking a dry piece of straw.

c One ancient translation I am; *Hebrew* Why am I.

²⁶ You bring bitter charges against me;
    even for what I did when I was young.
²⁷ You bind chains on my feet;
    you watch every step and even examine
      my footprints.
²⁸ As a result, I crumble like rotten wood,
    like a moth-eaten coat.

14   All men lead the same short, troubled
      life.
² They grow and wither as quickly as flowers;
    they disappear like shadows.
³ Will you even look at me, God,
    or bring me before you to be judged?
⁴ Nothing clean can ever come
    from anything as unclean as man.
⁵ The length of his life is decided before-
    hand—
    the number of months he will live.
You have settled it, and it can't be changed.
⁶ Look away from him and leave him alone;
    let him enjoy his life of hard work.

⁷ There is hope for a tree that has been cut
      down;
    it can come back to life and sprout.
⁸ Even though its roots grow old,
    and its stump dies in the ground,
⁹   with water it will sprout like a young
      plant.
¹⁰ But a man dies, and that is the end of him;
    he dies, and where is he then?

¹¹ A time will come when rivers stop run-
      ning,
    and even the seas go dry.
¹² But dead men will never rise;
    they will never wake up while the skies
      last;
    they will never stir out of their sleep.

¹³ I wish you would hide me alive in the land
   of the dead;*d*

   let me be hidden until your anger is
   over,

   and then set a time to remember me.

¹⁴ If a man dies, can he come back to life?
   But I will wait for better times,

   wait till this time of trouble is over.

¹⁵ Then you will call and I will answer,

   and you will be pleased with me, your
   creature.

¹⁶ Then you will watch every step I take,

   but you will not keep track of my sins.

¹⁷ You will forgive my sins and put them
   away;

   you will wipe out all the wrongs I have
   done.

¹⁸ A time will come when mountains fall,

   and even rock cliffs are moved away.

¹⁹ Water will wear down rocks,

   and hard rain wash away the soil;

   so you destroy man's hope for life.

²⁰ You overpower a man and send him away
   forever;

   his face is twisted in death.

²¹ His sons win honor, but he never knows
   it,

   nor is he told when they are disgraced.

²² He feels only the pain of his own body

   and the grief of his own mind.

d LAND OF THE DEAD: See 10.21.

The Second Dialogue

(15.1—21.34)

15

Eliphaz

1-2 Empty words, Job! Empty words!

3 No wise man would talk the way you do,
   or defend himself with such meaning-
   less words.

4 You discourage people from fearing God;
   you keep them from praying to him.

5 Your guilty conscience is speaking now;
   you are trying to hide behind clever
   words.

6 There is no need for me to condemn you;
   you are condemned by every word you
   speak.

7 Do you think you were the first man born?
   Were you there when God made the
   mountains?

8 Did you overhear the plans God made?
   - Does human wisdom belong to you
   alone?

9 There is nothing you know that we don't
   know.

10 We learned our wisdom from gray-headed
   men—
   men born before your father was.

11 God offers you comfort; why still reject it?
   We have spoken for him with calm,
   even words.

12 But you are excited and glare at us in
   anger.

13 You are angry with God and denounce
   'him.

¹⁴ Can any man be really pure?
    Can anyone be right with God?
¹⁵ Why, God does not even trust his angels;
    even they are not pure in his sight.
¹⁶ And man drinks evil as if it were water;
    yes, man is corrupt; man is worthless.

¹⁷ Now listen, Job, to what I know.
¹⁸ Wise men have taught me truths
    which they learned from their fathers,
    and they kept no secrets hidden.
¹⁹ Since their land was free from foreigners,
    there was no one to lead them away
        from God.

²⁰ A wicked man who oppresses others
    will be in trouble as long as he lives.
²¹ Voices of terror will scream in his ears,
    and robbers attack when he thinks he is
        safe.
²² He has no hope of escaping from dark-
        ness,
    for somewhere a sword is waiting to kill
        him,
²³   and vultures^e are waiting to eat his
        body.
    He knows his future is dark;
²⁴   disaster, like a powerful king,
    is waiting to attack him.

²⁵ That is the fate of the man
    who shakes his fist at God,
    and defies the Almighty.
²⁶⁻²⁷ That man is proud and rebellious;
    he stubbornly holds up his shield
    and rushes to fight against God.

e One ancient translation vultures; _Hebrew_ where is he?

²⁸ That is the man who captured cities
    and seized houses whose owners had
    fled,
    but war will destroy those cities and
    houses.
²⁹ He will not be rich long;
    nothing he owns will last.
Even his shadow[f] will vanish,
³⁰   and he will not escape from darkness.
He will be like a tree
    whose branches are burned by fire,
    whose blossoms[g] are blown away by the
    wind.
³¹ If he is foolish enough to trust in wicked-
    ness
    then wickedness will be all he gets.
³² Before his time is up he will wither,[h]
    wither like a branch and never be green
    again.
³³ He will be like a vine that loses its grapes
    before they are ripe;
    like an olive tree that never bears fruit.
³⁴ There will be no descendants for godless
    men,
    and fire will destroy the homes built by
    bribery.
³⁵ These are the men who plan trouble and
    do evil;
    their hearts are always full of deceit.

16

Job

¹⁻² I have heard words like that before;
    the comfort you give is only torment.
³ Are you going to keep on talking forever?
    Do you always have to have the last
    word?

---

f *One ancient translation* shadow; *Hebrew unclear.* g *One ancient translation* blossoms; *Hebrew* mouth. h *Some ancient translations* wither; *Hebrew* be filled.

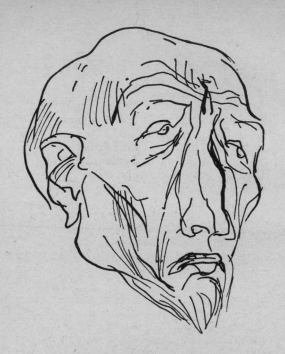

⁴ If you were in my place and I in yours,
      I could say everything you are saying.
   I could shake my head wisely
      and drown you with a flood of words.
⁵ I could strengthen you with advice
      and keep talking to comfort you.

⁶ But nothing I say helps,
      and being silent does not calm my pain.
⁷ You have worn me out, God;
      you have let my family be killed.
⁸   You have seized me. You are my en-
      emy.
   I am skin and bones,
      and people take that as proof of my
      guilt.ⁱ

ⁱ *Verses 7-8 in Hebrew are unclear.*

⁹ In anger, God tears me limb from limb;
    he glares at me with hate.
¹⁰ People sneer at me;
    they crowd around me and slap my face.
¹¹ God has turned me over to evil men.
¹² I was living in peace,
    but God took me by the throat
    and battered me and crushed me.
God uses me for target practice
¹³   and shoots arrows at me from every
      side—
    arrows that pierce and wound me;
    and even then he shows no pity.
¹⁴ He wounds me again and again;
    he attacks like a soldier gone mad with
      hate.

¹⁵ I mourn and wear clothes made of sack-
    cloth,ʲ
    and I sit here in the dust defeated.
¹⁶ I have cried until my face is red,
    and my eyes are swollen and circled
      with shadows,
¹⁷   but I have not committed any violence,
    and my prayer to God is sincere.

¹⁸ Earth, don't hide the wrongs done to me!
    Don't let my call for justice be silenced!
¹⁹ There is someone in heaven
    to stand up for me and take my side.
²⁰ I want God to see my tears and hear my
    prayer.ᵏ

²¹ I want someone to plead with God for me,
    as a man pleads for his friend.
²² My years are passing now,
    and I walk the road of no return.

ʲ SACKCLOTH: Coarse cloth used to make clothes worn by persons who were mourning. ᵏ *One ancient translation* and hear my prayer; *Hebrew unclear.*

17 The end of my life is near. I can hardly
　　　breathe;
　　　　there is nothing left for me but the
　　　　grave.
² I watch how bitterly people mock me.
³ I am honest, God. Accept my word.
　　　There is no one else to support what I
　　　say.
⁴ You have closed their minds to reason;
　　　don't let them gloat over me now.
⁵ In the old proverb a man betrays his
　　　friends for money,
　　　and his children suffer for it.
⁶ And now they use this proverb against me;
　　　people hear it and come and spit in my
　　　face.
⁷ My grief has almost made me blind;
　　　my arms and legs are as thin as shadows.
⁸ Those who claim to be honest are shocked,
　　　and they all condemn me as godless.
⁹ Those who claim to be respectable
　　　are more and more convinced they are
　　　right.
¹⁰ But if all of them came and stood before
　　　me,
　　　I would not find even one of them wise.

¹¹ My days have passed; my plans have
　　　failed;
　　　my hope is gone.
¹² But my friends say night is daylight;
　　　they say that light is near,
　　　but I still remain in darkness.
¹³ My only hope is the world of the dead,[l]
　　　where I will lie down to sleep in the
　　　dark.
¹⁴ I will say that the grave is my father,
　　　and the worms that eat me are my
　　　mother and sisters.

---

l WORLD OF THE DEAD: See 10.21.

¹⁵ Where is there any hope for me? Who
      sees any?
¹⁶ Hope will not go with me^m
      when I go to the world of the dead.ⁿ

24

Bildad
¹⁻² Job, can people like you never be quiet?
      If you stopped to listen we could talk to
      you.
³ What makes you think we are as stupid as
      cattle?
⁴ You are only hurting yourself with your
      anger.
      Will the earth be deserted because of
      you?
      Will mountains be moved because of
      you?

m One ancient translation with me; *Hebrew unclear. n* WORLD OF THE
DEAD: See 10.21.

⁵ The wicked man's light will be put out;
    its flame will never burn again.
⁶ The lamp in his tent will be darkened.
⁷ His steps were firm, but now he limps;
    he falls—a victim of his own advice.
⁸ He walks into a net and his feet are
    caught;
⁹   a trap catches his heels and holds him.
¹⁰ On the ground a snare is hidden for him;
    a trap has been set in his path.

¹¹ All around him terror is waiting;
    it follows him at every step.
¹² He used to be rich, but now he goes hun-
    gry;
    disaster stands and waits at his side.
¹³ A deadly disease spreads over his body,
    and causes his arms and legs to rot.
¹⁴ He is torn from the tent where he lived
    secure,
    and is dragged off to face King Death.
¹⁵ Now anyone may live in his tent—
    after sulfur is sprinkled to disinfect it!ᵒ
¹⁶ His roots and branches are withered and
    dry.
¹⁷ His fame is ended at home and abroad;
    no one remembers him any more.
¹⁸ He will be driven out of the land of the
    living,
    driven from light into darkness.
¹⁹ He has no descendants, no survivors.
²⁰ From east to west, everyone who hears of
    his fate
    shudders and trembles with fear.
²¹ This is the fate of evil men,
    the fate of those who care nothing for
    God.

ᵒ TO DISINFECT IT: Sulfur was used in the ancient world as a dis-
infectant and to clean rooms that had contained corpses.

19

Job

1-2 Why do you keep tormenting me with
      words?
 3 Time after time you insult me,
      and show no shame for the way you
      abuse me.
 4 Suppose I have done wrong. How does
      that hurt you?
 5 You think you are better than I am,
      and regard my trouble as proof of my
      guilt.
 6 Can't you see it is God who has done this?
      He has set a trap to catch me.
 7 I protest his violence, but no one listens;
      I call for justice, but there isn't any.
 8 God has blocked the way, and I can't get
      through;
      he has covered my path with darkness.
 9 He has taken away all my wealth,
      and destroyed my reputation.

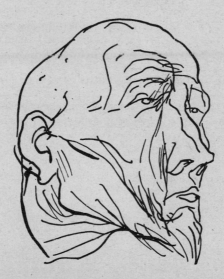

¹⁰ He batters me from every side.
   He uproots my hope
      and leaves me to wither and die.
¹¹ God is angry and rages against me;
      and treats me like his worst enemy.
¹² He sends his army to attack me;
      they dig trenches and lay siege to my
      tent.

¹³ God has made my brothers forsake me;
      I am a stranger to those who knew me;
¹⁴   my relatives and friends are gone.
¹⁵ Those who were guests in my house have
      forgotten me;
      my housemaids treat me like a stranger
      and a foreigner.
¹⁶ When I call a servant he doesn't answer—
      even when I beg him to help me.
¹⁷ My wife can't stand the smell of my
      breath,
      and my own brothers won't come near
      me.
¹⁸ Children despise me and laugh when they
      see me.
¹⁹ My closest friends look at me with disgust;
      those I loved most have turned against
      me.
²⁰ My skin hangs loose on my bones;
      I have barely escaped with my life.ᵖ
²¹ You are my friends! Take pity on me!
      The hand of God has struck me down.
²² Why must you persecute me the way God
      does?
      Haven't you tormented me enough?

²³ How I wish someone would record what I
      am saying,
      and write my words in a book!
²⁴ Or with a chisel carve my words in stone,
      and write them so they would last for-
      ever.

ᵖ Hebrew unclear.

²⁵ But I know there is someone in heaven
    who will come at last to my defense.
²⁶ Even after my skin is eaten by disease,
    in this body I will see God.�q
²⁷ I will see him with my own eyes,
    and he will not be a stranger.

   My courage failed because you men said,
²⁸   "How can we torment him?"
    You looked for some excuse to attack
      me.
²⁹ But now, be afraid of the sword—
    the sword that brings God's wrath on
      sin,
    so that you will know there is one who
      judges.

20

Zophar
¹⁻²Job, you upset me. Now I'm impatient to
    answer.
³   What you have said is an insult,
    but I know how to reply to you.

⁴ Surely you know that from ancient times,
    when man was first placed on earth,
⁵   no wicked man has been happy for long.
⁶ He may grow great and tower to the sky,
    be so great his head reaches the clouds,
⁷   but he will be blown away like dust.
   Those who used to know him
    will wonder where he has gone.
⁸ He will vanish like a dream, like a vision
    at night,
    and never be seen again.
⁹ He will disappear from the place where he
    used to live;
¹⁰   and his sons will make good what he
    stole from the poor.

�q *Verse 26 in Hebrew is unclear.*

¹¹ His body used to be young and vigorous,
but soon it will turn to dust.

¹²⁻¹³ Evil tastes so good to him
he keeps some in his mouth to enjoy the
taste.

¹⁴ But in his stomach this food turns bitter,
as bitter as any poison could be.

¹⁵ The wicked man vomits up the wealth he
stole;
God takes it back, even out of his stom-
ach.

¹⁶ What the evil man swallows is like poison;
it kills him like the bite of a deadly
snake.

¹⁷ He will not live to see rivers of olive oil,^r
or streams that flow with milk and
honey.

¹⁸ He will have to give up all he has worked
for;
he will have no chance to enjoy his
wealth,

¹⁹ because he oppressed and neglected the
poor,
and seized houses someone else had
built.

^r *Hebrew unclear.*

20 His greed is never satisfied.
21 When he eats, there is nothing left over,
   but now his prosperity comes to an end.
22 At the height of his success,
   all the weight of misery will crush him.
23 Let him eat all he wants!
   God will punish him in fury and anger.
24 When he tries to escape from an iron
      sword,
   a bronze bow will shoot him down.
25 An arrow sticks through his body;
   its shiny point drips with his blood,
   and terror grips his heart.
26 Everything he has saved is destroyed;
   a fire not lit by human hands
   burns him and all his family.
27 Heaven reveals this man's sin,
   and the earth gives testimony against
      him.
28 All his wealth will be destroyed
   in the flood of God's anger.

29 This is the fate of wicked men,
   the fate that God decrees for them.

21

Job

1-2 Listen to what I am saying;
   that is all the comfort I ask from you.
3 Give me a chance to speak and then,
   when I am through, sneer if you like.

4 My quarrel is not with mortal men;
   I have good reason to be impatient.
5 Look at me. Isn't that enough
   to make you stare in shocked silence?
6 When I think of what has happened to me,
   I am stunned, and I tremble and shake.

⁷ Why does God let evil men grow old and
     prosper?
⁸ Their children and grandchildren
     grow up before their very eyes.
⁹ God does not bring disaster on their
     homes;
     they never have to live in terror.
¹⁰ Yes, all their cattle breed
     and give birth without trouble.
¹¹ Their children run and play like lambs
¹²   and dance to the music of harps and
     flutes.
¹³ They live out their lives in peace,
     and die quietly without suffering.

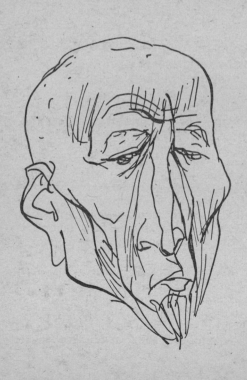

14 The wicked tell God to leave them alone;
    they don't want to know his will for
        their lives.
15 They think there is no need to serve God,
    or any advantage in praying to him.
16 They claim they succeed by their own
        strength,
    but their way of thinking I can't accept.

17 Was a wicked man's light ever put out?
        Did one of them ever meet with dis-
            aster?
    Did God ever punish the wicked in anger
18   and make them like straw blown by the
            wind
        or like dust carried away in a storm?

19 You claim God punishes a child for the
        sins of his father.
    No! Let God punish the sinners them-
        selves,
        and show he does it because of their
            sins.
20 Let sinners bear their own punishment;
        let them feel the wrath of Almighty
            God.
21 When a man's life is over,
        does he really care if his children are
            happy?
22 Can a man teach God?
    Can a man judge Almighty God?

23-24 Some men stay healthy till the day they
            die;
        they die happy and at ease,
        and their bodies are well-nourished.
25 Others have no happiness at all;
        they live and die with bitter hearts.
26 But all alike die and are buried;
        they all are covered with worms.

²⁷ I know what spiteful things you think.
²⁸ You ask, "Where is the house of the great
     man now,
        the man who practiced evil?"

²⁹ Haven't you talked with people who
     travel?
        Don't you know the reports they bring
        back?
³⁰ On the day when God is angry and pun-
     ishes,
        it is the wicked man who is always
        spared.
³¹ There is no one to accuse a wicked man,
        or pay him back for all he has done.
³² When he is carried to the graveyard,
        to where his tomb is guarded,
³³   thousands join the funeral procession,
        and even the earth lies gently on his
        body.

³⁴ And you! You try to comfort me with
     nonsense!
        Everything you have said is a lie!

The Third Dialogue

(22.1—27.23)

22

Eliphaz
¹⁻² Is there any man, even the wisest,
        who could ever be of use to God?
³ Does your doing right benefit God,
        or does your being good help him?
⁴ It is not because you fear God
        that he reprimands you and brings you
        to trial.
⁵ No, it's because you have sinned so much,
        and because of all the evil you do.

⁶ To make your brother pay you the money
        he owed,
      you took away his clothes and left him
        nothing to wear.
⁷ You refused water to those who were
        tired,
      and refused to feed those who were
        hungry.
⁸ You used your power and your position
      to take over the whole land.
⁹ You not only refused to help widows,
      but you also robbed and mistreated or-
        phans.
¹⁰ So now there are pitfalls all around you,
      and suddenly you are full of fear.
¹¹ It has grown so dark you cannot see,
      and a flood overwhelms you.

¹² Doesn't God live in the highest heavens
      and look down on the stars, even though
        they are high?
¹³ And yet you ask, "What does God know?
      He is covered by clouds—how can he
        judge us?"
¹⁴ You think the thick clouds keep him from
        seeing,
      as he walks on the boundary between
        earth and sky.ˢ

¹⁵ Is your mind made up to walk in the paths
      that evil men have always followed?
¹⁶ Even before their time had come,
      a flood washed them away.
¹⁷ These are the men who rejected God
      and believed that he could do nothing
        to them.
¹⁸ And yet it was God who made them pros-
        perous—
      I can't understand the thoughts of the
        wicked.

ˢ BOUNDARY BETWEEN EARTH AND SKY: The horizon seemed to be a
great circle where the earth met the sky. It was thought that God
inspected the earth by walking around it on the horizon.

¹⁹ Good men are glad and innocent men
      laugh
      when they see the wicked punished.
²⁰ All that the wicked own*t* is destroyed,
      and fire burns up anything that is left.

²¹ Now, Job, make peace with God
      and stop treating him like an enemy;
      if you do, then he will bless you.
²² Accept the teaching he gives;
      keep his words in your heart.
²³ Yes, you must humbly*u* return to God,
      and put an end to all the evil
      that is done in your house.
²⁴ Throw away your gold;
      dump your finest gold in the dry stream
      bed.
²⁵ Let Almighty God be your gold
      and let him be silver, piled high for you.
²⁶ Then you will always trust in God
      and find that he is the source of your
      joy.
²⁷ When you pray, he will answer you,
      and you will keep the vows you made.
²⁸ You will succeed in all you do,
      and light will shine on your path.
²⁹ God brings down the proud*v*
      and saves the humble.
³⁰ He will rescue you if you are innocent,
      if what you do is right.*w*

23

Job

¹⁻² I still rebel and complain against God;
      I cannot keep from groaning.
   ³ How I wish I knew where to find him,
      and knew how to go where he is.

---

t One ancient translation own; *Hebrew unclear.* *u One ancient translation* humbly; *Hebrew* be built up. *v* proud; *Hebrew unclear.* *w Verse
30 in Hebrew is unclear.*

⁴ I would state my case before him,
    and present all the arguments in my
    favor.
⁵ I want to know what he would say,
    and how he would answer me.
⁶ Would God use all his strength against me?
    No, he would listen as I spoke.
⁷ I am honest; I could reason with God;
    he would declare me innocent once and
    for all.

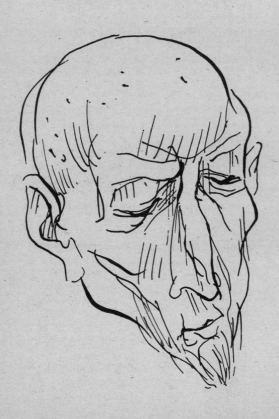

⁸ I have searched in the East, but God is
    not there;
    and I have not found him when I
    searched in the West.
⁹ God has been at work in the North,
    and he has traveled to the South,
    but still I have not seen him.
¹⁰ Yet God knows every step I take;
    if he tests me he will find me pure.
¹¹ I follow faithfully the road he chooses,
    and I never wander to either side.
¹² I always do what God commands;
    I follow his will, not my own desires.

¹³ He never changes. No one can oppose
    him,
    or keep him from doing what he wants
    to do.
¹⁴ He will fulfill what he has planned for me;
    that plan is only one of the many he
    has,
¹⁵   and I tremble with fear before him.
¹⁶⁻¹⁷ Almighty God has destroyed my courage,
    It is God, not the darkness, that makes me
    afraid—
    even though the dark blinds my eyes.

24 Why doesn't God set a time for judging,
    a day of justice for those who serve him?

² Men move boundary markersˣ to get more
    land;
    they steal sheep and put them with their
    own flocks.
³ They steal donkeys that belong to orphans,
    and keep a widow's ox till she pays her
    debts.
⁴ They keep the poor from getting their
    rights
    and force the needy to run and hide.

ˣ MOVE BOUNDARY MARKERS: Stones were set up to show the boundary
between one person's property and that of his neighbor, but a dis-
honest person could move the stones and get more land.

⁵ So the poor, like wild donkeys,
    search for food in the dry wilderness;
        nowhere else can they find food for
        their children.
⁶ They have to harvest fields they don't own,ʸ
    and gather grapes in wicked men's vine-
        yards.
⁷ At night they sleep with nothing to cover
        them,
    nothing to keep them from the cold.
⁸ They are drenched by the rain that falls on
        the mountains,
    and they huddle beside the rocks for
        shelter

⁹ Evil men make slaves of fatherless infants,
    and take the poor man's children in
        payment for debts.
¹⁰ But the poor must go out with no clothes
        to protect them;
    they must go hungry while harvesting
        wheat.
¹¹ They press olives for oil, and grapes for
        wine,
    but they themselves are thirsty.
¹² In the city you hear the cries of the
        wounded and dying,
    but God ignores their prayers.

¹³ There are men who reject the light;
    they don't understand it and avoid its
        paths.
¹⁴ At dawn the murderer goes out to kill the
        poor,
    and at night he robs.

ʸ FIELDS THEY DON'T OWN: Having been cheated out of their own land,
the poor are forced to work for others for very small pay.

¹⁵ The adulterer waits for twilight to come
and hides his face so no one can see
him.
¹⁶ At night thieves break into houses,
but by day they hide and avoid the
light.
¹⁷ They fear the light of day,
but darkness holds no terror for them.

[*Zophar*]^z
¹⁸ The wicked man is swept away by floods,
and the land he owns is under God's
curse;
he no longer goes to work in his vine-
yards.
¹⁹ As snow vanishes in heat and drought,
so a sinner vanishes from the land of
the living.
²⁰ No one remembers him, not even his
mother;
worms eat him; he is completely destroyed.
²¹ This happens because he mistreated wid-
ows
and showed no kindness to childless
women.
²² God, in his strength, destroys the mighty;
he acts and the wicked man dies.
²³ God may let him live secure,
but keeps an eye on him all the time.
²⁴ For a while the wicked man succeeds
but then he withers like a weed,
like a stalk of grain that has been cut
down.
²⁵ Can anyone deny that this is so?
Can anyone prove that my words are not
true?

z Zophar *is not named in the text, but this speech is usually assigned
to him.*

25

Bildad

¹⁻² God is powerful; all must fear him;
      he keeps his heavenly kingdom in peace.
³ Can anyone count the angels who serve
      him?
  Is there any place where God's light does
      not shine?
⁴ Can anyone be righteous or pure in God's
      eyes?
⁵ In his eyes even the moon is not bright,
      or the stars pure.
⁶ Then what about man, that worm, that in-
      sect?
  What is man worth in God's eyes?

26

Job

1-2 What a help you are in rescuing me—
    poor, weak man that I am!
3 You give such good advice
    and share your knowledge with a fool
    like me!
4 Who do you think will hear all your
    words?
    Who inspired you to speak like this?

[*Bildad*]*a*

5 The land of the dead is trembling;
    its inhabitants shake with fear.
6 The world of the dead*b* lies open to God;
    no covering shields it from his sight.
7 God stretched out the northern sky,
    and hung the earth in empty space.
8 It is God who fills the clouds with water,
    and keeps them from bursting with the
    weight.
9 He hides the full moon behind a cloud.
10 He divided light from darkness
    by a circle drawn on the face of the
    ocean.
11 When he threatens the pillars*c* that hold
    up the sky,
    they shake and tremble with fear.
12 It is his strength that conquered the sea;*d*
    by his skill he destroyed the monster
    Rahab.*e*
13 It is his breath that made the sky clear,
    and his hand that killed the escaping
    monster.*f*
14 But these are only hints of his power,
    only the whispers that we have heard.
    Who can know how truly great God is?

a Bildad *is not named in the text, but this speech is usually credited to him.* *b* WORLD OF THE DEAD: See 10.21. *c* PILLARS: See 9.6. *d* CONQUERED THE SEA: A reference to an ancient story in which the sea fought against God. *e* RAHAB: See 9.13. *f* ESCAPING MONSTER: See 9.8.

27

Job

¹⁻² I swear by the living Almighty God,
    who refuses me justice and makes my
       life bitter—
³   as long as God gives me breath
⁴   my lips will never say anything evil,
    and my tongue will never speak a lie.
⁵ I will never say that you men are right;
    as long as I live I will insist I am inno-
       cent.
⁶ I will never give up my claim to be right;
    my conscience is clear.

⁷ May all who oppose me and fight against
       me
    be punished like wicked, unrighteous
       men.
⁸ What hope is there for godless men
    in the hour when God demands their
       life?
⁹ When trouble comes, will God hear their
       cries?
¹⁰ They should have wanted the joy he gives
    and should have constantly prayed to
       him.

¹¹ Let me teach you how great is God's
       power,
    and explain what Almighty God has
       planned.
¹² But no, after all, you have seen for your-
       selves;
    so why do you talk such nonsense?

[*Zophar*]*g*

¹³ Here is how Almighty God punishes
    wicked, violent men.
¹⁴ They may have many sons, but all are
    killed in war;
    their children never have enough to eat.
¹⁵ Those who survive will die from disease,
    and their widows will not mourn their
    death.
¹⁶ The wicked may have too much silver to
    count,
    and more clothes than anyone needs.
¹⁷ But some good man will wear the clothes,
    and some honest man will get the silver.
¹⁸ The wicked build houses that will not last;
    they are like a spider's web,
    or the hut of a slave guarding the fields.
¹⁹ One last time*h* they will lie down rich,
    and when they wake up they will find
    their wealth gone.
²⁰ Terror will strike like a sudden flood;
    a wind in the night will blow them away;
²¹   the east wind will sweep them from
    their homes;
²²   it will blow down on them without pity,
    while they try their best to escape.
²³ The wind howls at them as they run,
    frightening them with destructive power.

In Praise of Wisdom*i*

28   There are mines where silver is dug;
    There are places where gold is refined.
  ² Men dig iron out of the ground
    And melt copper out of the stones.
  ³ Men explore the deepest darkness.
    They search the depths of the earth
    And dig for rocks in the darkness.

g Zophar *is not named in the text, but this speech is usually credited
to him.* *h* Some ancient translations *One last time;* Hebrew *They will
not be gathered.* *i* The Hebrew text does not indicate who is speaking
in this chapter.

⁴ Far from where anyone lives,
  Or human feet ever travel,
  Men dig the shafts of mines.
  There they work in loneliness,
  Clinging to ropes in the pits.

⁵ Food grows out of the earth,
  But underneath the same earth
  All is torn up and crushed.
⁶ The stones of the earth contain sapphires,ⁱ
  And the dust contains gold.
⁷ No hawk sees the roads to the mines
  And no vulture ever flies over them.
⁸ No lion or other fierce beast
  Ever travels those lonely roads.

⁹ Men dig the hardest rocks,
  Dig mountains away at their base.
¹⁰ As they tunnel through the rocks
  They discover precious stones.
¹¹ They dig to the sources ofᵏ rivers
  And bring to light what is hidden.
¹² But where is the source of wisdom?
  Where can we learn to understand?

¹³ Wisdom is not to be found among men;
  No one knows its true value.
¹⁴ The depths of the oceans and seas
  Say that wisdom is not found there.
¹⁵ It cannot be bought with silver or gold.
¹⁶ The finest gold and jewels
  Cannot pay its price.
¹⁷ Its value is more than gold,
  Than a gold vase or finest glass.
¹⁸ The value of wisdom is more
  Than coral,ˡ or crystal,ᵐ or rubies.ⁿ

ⁱ SAPPHIRE: A precious stone, usually blue in color. ᵏ *Some ancient translations* dig to the sources of; *Hebrew* bind from trickling. ˡ CORAL: A stony substance found in the sea which is used to make jewelry. ᵐ CRYSTAL: A semiprecious stone, usually clear and colorless. ⁿ RUBY: A precious stone, deep-red in color.

¹⁹ The finest topaz° and the purest gold
   Cannot compare with the value of wisdom.

²⁰ Where, then, is the source of wisdom?
   Where can we learn to understand?
²¹ No living creature can see it,
   Not even a bird in flight.
²² Even death and destruction
   Admit they have heard only rumors.

²³ God alone knows the way,
   Knows the place where wisdom is found,
²⁴ Because he sees the ends of the earth,
   Sees everything under the sky.
²⁵ When God gave the wind its power,
   And determined the size of the sea;
²⁶ When God decided where the rain would
      fall,
   And the path that the thunderclouds travel;
²⁷ It was then he saw wisdom and tested its
      value—
   He established it and gave his approval.

²⁸ God said to men,
   "To be wise, you must fear the Lord.
   To understand, you must turn from evil."

Job's Final Statement of His Case

29   Job began speaking again.

Job

² If only my life could be again
      as it was when God watched over me.
³ God was always with me then,
      and gave me light as I walked through
      the darkness.
⁴ Those were the days when I was prosper-
      ous,
      when God's friendship protected my
      home.

° TOPAZ: A semiprecious stone, usually yellow in color.

⁵ Almighty God was with me then,
   and I was surrounded by all my children.
⁶ My cows and goats gave plenty of milk,
   and my olive trees grew in the rockiest
   soil.
⁷ Whenever the city elders met,
   and I took my place among them,
⁸   young men stepped aside as soon as
   they saw me,
   and old men stood up to show me respect.
⁹ The leaders of the people would stop talking;
¹⁰   even the most important men kept
   silent.

¹¹ Everyone who saw me or heard about me
    had good things to say about what I had
    done.
¹² When the poor cried out, I helped them;
    I helped orphans who had nowhere to
    turn.
¹³ Men who were in deepest misery praised
    me,
    and I helped widows find security.
¹⁴ I have always acted justly and fairly.
¹⁵ I helped the blind and the lame.
¹⁶ I was like a father to the poor,
    and took the side of strangers in trouble.
¹⁷ I destroyed the power of cruel men
    and rescued their victims.

¹⁸ I always expected to live a long life,
    and to die at home in comfort.
¹⁹ I was like a tree whose roots always have
    water,
    and whose branches are wet with dew.
²⁰ Everyone was always praising me,
    and my strength never failed me.
²¹ When I gave advice, people were silent
    and listened carefully to what I said;
²²   they had nothing to add when I was
    through.
  My words sank in like drops of rain;
²³   everyone listened eagerly,
    the way farmers welcome the spring
    rains.
²⁴ When I smiled on them they could hardly
    believe it;
    their gloom never discouraged me.
²⁵ I took charge and made the decisions;
    I led them the way a king leads his
    troops,
    and gave them comfort when they were
    discouraged.

30 But men younger than I am make fun of
me now!
Their fathers have always been so worthless
I wouldn't let them help my dogs guard
sheep.
2 They were a bunch of worn-out men,
too weak to do any work for me.
3 They were so poor and hungry
they would gnaw dry roots—
at night, in wild, desolate places.[p]
4 They pulled up and ate the plants of the
desert,
even the tasteless roots of the broom
tree!
5 Everyone drove them away with shouts,
the way you shout at a thief.
6 They had to live in caves,
in holes dug in the sides of cliffs.
7 Out in the wilds they howled like animals,
and huddled together under the bushes.
8 A worthless bunch of nameless nobodies!
They were driven out of the land.

9 Now they come and laugh at me;
I am nothing but a joke to them.
10 They treat me with disgust;
they think they are too good for me,
and even come and spit in my face.
11 Because God has made me weak and helpless,
they turn against me with all their fury.
12 This mob attacks me head-on;
they send me running; they prepare
their final assault.
13 They cut off my escape and try to destroy
me;
and there is no one to stop[q] them.

[p] at night, in wild, desolate places; *Hebrew unclear.* [q] stop; *Hebrew* help.

¹⁴ They pour through the holes in my
defenses,
    and come crashing down on top of me;
¹⁵ I am overcome with terror.
My dignity is gone like a puff of wind,
    and my prosperity like a cloud.

¹⁶ Now I am about to die;
    there is no relief for my suffering.
¹⁷ At night my bones all ache;
    the pain that gnaws me never stops.
¹⁸ God grabs me by my collar
    and twists my clothes out of shape.
¹⁹ He throws me down in the mud;
    I am no better than dirt.

²⁰ I call to you, God, but you never answer;
    and when I pray, you pay no attention.
²¹ You are treating me cruelly;
    you persecute me with all your power.
²² You let the wind blow me away;
    you toss me about in a raging storm.
²³ I know you are taking me off to my death,
    to the fate in store for everyone.
²⁴ Why do you attack a ruined man
    who can do nothing but beg for pity?[r]
²⁵ Didn't I weep with people in trouble
    and feel sorry for those in need?
²⁶ I hoped for happiness and light,
    but trouble and darkness came instead.
²⁷ I am torn apart by worry and pain;
    there is nothing but suffering ahead.
²⁸ I walk in gloom and there is no comfort;[s]
    I stand up in public and plead for help.
²⁹ My voice is as sad and lonely
    as the cries of a jackal[t] or an ostrich.
³⁰ My skin has turned dark; I am burning
    with fever.
³¹ Where once I heard joyful music,
    there is now only mourning and weep-
    ing.

[r] Verse 24 in Hebrew is unclear. [s] comfort; Hebrew sun. [t] JACKAL:
A dog-like wild animal noted for its appetite.

31 I have made a solemn promise
          never to look at a girl with lust.

² What does Almighty God do to us?
     How does he repay human deeds?
³ He sends disaster and ruin
     to those who do wrong.
⁴ God knows everything I do;
     he sees every step I take.

⁵ I swear I have never acted wickedly,
     and never tried to deceive others.
⁶ Let God weigh me on honest scales,
     and he will see how innocent I am.
⁷ If I have turned from the right path,
     or let myself be attracted to evil,
     if my hands are stained with sin,
⁸   then let my crops be destroyed,
     or let others eat the food I grow.

⁹ If I have been attracted to my neighbor's
          wife,
     and waited, hidden, outside her door,
¹⁰   then let my wife fix another man's food
     and sleep in another man's bed.
[¹¹ Such a sin would be wicked and would be punished by death. ¹² It would be like a destructive, hellish
fire, destroying everything I have.]

¹³ When one of my servants complained
          against me,
     I would listen and treat him fairly.
¹⁴ If I did not, how could I then face God?
     What could I say when God came to
          judge me?
¹⁵ The same God who created me
     created my servants also.

¹⁶ I have never refused to help the poor,
        never let widows live in despair,
¹⁷   or let orphans go hungry while I ate.
¹⁸ All my life I have taken care of them.

¹⁹ When I found someone in need, too poor
        to buy clothes,
²⁰   I would give him clothing made of wool
        that had come from my own flock of
        sheep.
And he would praise me with all his heart.

²¹ If I have ever cheated an orphan,
        because I knew I could win in court,
²²   then may my arms be broken;
        may they be torn out of my shoulders.
²³ Because I fear God's punishment,
        I could never do such a thing.

²⁴ I have never trusted in riches,
²⁵   or taken pride in my wealth.
²⁶ I have never worshiped the sun in its
        brightness,
        or the moon in all its beauty.
²⁷ I have never even been tempted to do it.
²⁸ Such a sin would be punished by death;
        it denies Almighty God.

²⁹ I have never been glad when my enemies
        suffered,
        or pleased when they met with disaster;
³⁰   I never sinned by praying for their
        death.
³¹ All the men who work for me know
        that I have always welcomed strangers.
³² I have welcomed travelers into my home,
        and never let them sleep in the streets.

33 Other men try to hide their sins,
    but I have never concealed mine.
34 I have never feared what people would
        say;
    I have never kept quiet or stayed in-
        doors
    because I feared their scorn.

35 Will no one listen to what I am saying?
    I swear that every word is true.
    Let Almighty God answer me.

    If the charges my opponent brings against
        me
        were written down so that I could have
            them,
36   I would wear them proudly around my
            neck,
        and hold them up for everyone to see.
37 I would tell God everything I have done,
        and hold my head high in his presence.

38 If I have stolen the land I farm
    and taken it from its rightful owners—
39   if I have eaten the food that grew,
        but let the farmers that grew it starve—
40   then instead of wheat and barley
        may weeds and thistles grow.

The words of Job are ended.

The Speeches of Elihu

(32.4—37.24)

32 The three men stopped trying to answer Job,
    because he was convinced of his own inno-
cence. 2 Then a man named Elihu could not control
his anger any longer, because Job justified himself and

blamed God. (Elihu was the son of Barakel, a descendant of Buz, and belonged to the clan of Ram.) ³ He was also angry with Job's three friends. They could not find any way to answer Job, and this made it appear that God was in the wrong. ⁴ Because Elihu was the youngest one there, he had waited until everyone finished speaking. ⁵ But when he saw that the three men could not answer Job, he was angry ⁶ and began to speak.

Elihu

I am young, and you are old,
so I was afraid to tell you what I think.
⁷ I told myself that you ought to speak,
that you older men should share your
wisdom.
⁸ But it is the spirit of Almighty God
that comes to men and gives them
wisdom.
⁹ It is not growing old that makes men wise,
or helps them know what is right.
¹⁰ So now I want you to listen to me;
let me tell you what I think.

¹¹ I listened patiently while you were speaking
and waited while you searched for wise
comments.
¹² I paid close attention and heard you fail;
you have not disproved what Job has
said.
¹³ How can you claim that you have discovered wisdom?
God must answer Job, for you have
failed.
¹⁴ Job was speaking to you, not to me,
but I would never answer the way you
did.

¹⁵ Words have failed them, Job;
they have no answer for you.

¹⁶ Shall I go on waiting, when they are silent?
　　They stand there with nothing more to
　　say.
¹⁷ No, I will give my own answer now,
　　and tell you what I think.
¹⁸ I can hardly wait to speak.
　　I can't hold back the words.
¹⁹ If I don't get a chance to speak,
　　I will burst like a wineskin full of new
　　wine.
²⁰ I can't stand it. I have to speak.
²¹ I will not take sides in this debate;
　　I am not going to flatter anyone.
²² I don't know how to flatter,
　　and God would quickly punish me if
　　I did.

32

And now, Job, listen carefully
　　to all that I have to say.
² I am going to say what's on my mind.
³ All my words are sincere,
　　and I am speaking the truth.
⁴ God's spirit made me and gave me life.

⁵ Answer me, if you can. Prepare your
　　arguments.
⁶ You and I, Job, are the same in God's
　　sight,
　　both of us were formed from clay.
⁷ So you have no reason to fear me;
　　I will not overpower you.

⁸ Now here is what I heard you say:
⁹ "I am not guilty. I have done nothing
　　wrong.
　　I am innocent and free from sin.
¹⁰ But God finds excuses for attacking me
　　and treats me like an enemy.
¹¹ He binds chains on my feet;
　　he watches every move I make."

¹² But I tell you, Job, you are wrong.
    God is greater than any man.
¹³ Why do you accuse God
    of never answering a man's complaints?
¹⁴ Even though God speaks in many ways,
    no one pays attention to what he says.
¹⁵ God speaks in dreams and visions
    that come at night when men are asleep.
¹⁶ God makes them listen to what he says,
    and they are frightened at his warnings.
¹⁷ God speaks to make them stop their sin-
    ning
    and to keep them from becoming proud.
¹⁸ God will not let them be destroyed;
    he saves them from death itself.
¹⁹ God corrects a man by sending sickness
    and filling his body with pain.
²⁰ The sick man loses his appetite,
    and even the finest food looks revolting.
²¹ His body wastes away; you can see all his
    bones;
²²   he is about to go to the world of the
    dead.

²³ Perhaps an angel may come to his aid—
    one of God's thousands of angels,
    who remind men of their duty.
²⁴ The angel, in mercy, will say, "Release
    him!
    He is not to go down to the world of
    the dead.
    Here is the ransom to set him free."
²⁵ His body will grow young and strong
    again;
²⁶   God will answer him when he prays;
    he will worship God with joy;
    God will make things right for him
    again.
²⁷ He will say in public, "I have sinned.
    I have not done right, but God spared
    me.

28 He kept me from going to the land of the
     dead,"
     and I am still alive."

29 God does all this again and again;
30   he saves the life of a person,
       and gives him the joy of living.

31 Now, Job, listen to what I am saying;
     be quiet and let me speak.
32 But if you have something to say, let me
     hear it;
       I would gladly admit you are in the
       right.
33 But if not, be quiet and listen to me,
     and I will teach you how to be wise.

34

Elihu

1-2 You men are so wise, so smart;
      listen now to what I am saying.
3 You can tell good food when you taste it;
    why can't you tell wise words when you
    hear them?
4 It is up to us to decide the case.
5 Job claims that he is innocent,
    and that God refuses to give him justice.
6 He asks, "How could I lie and say I am
    wrong?"
      I am fatally wounded, but I am sinless."

7 Have you ever seen anyone like this man
    Job?
      He never shows respect for God.
8 He likes the company of evil men
    and goes around with sinners.
9 He says that it never does any good
    to try to follow God's will.

" LAND OF THE DEAD: See 10.21   *v Hebrew unclear.*

¹⁰ You men understand. Listen to me.
    Will Almighty God do what is wrong?
¹¹ He rewards people for what they do
    and treats them the way they deserve.
¹² Almighty God does not do evil;
    he is never unjust to anyone.
¹³ Did God get his power from someone else?
    Did someone put him in charge of the
        world?
¹⁴ If God took back the breath of life,
¹⁵   then everyone living would die
    and turn into dust again.

¹⁶ Now listen to me, if you are wise.
¹⁷ Do you think the Almighty hates justice?
    Are you condemning the righteous God?
¹⁸ God condemns kings and rulers,
    when they are worthless or wicked.
¹⁹ God created everyone;
    he does not take the side of rulers,
    or favor the rich over the poor.
²⁰ A man may die suddenly at night.
    God strikes men down and they perish;
    he kills the mighty with no effort at all.
²¹ He watches every step men take.
²² There is no darkness dark enough
    to hide a sinner from God.
²³ God does not need to set a time^w
    for men to go and be judged by him.
²⁴ He does not need an investigation
    to remove leaders and replace them
        with others.
²⁵ Because he knows what they do,
    he overthrows them and crushes them
        by night.
²⁶ He punishes sinners where all can see it,
²⁷   because they have stopped following
        him
    and ignored all his commands.

_w_ a time; _Hebrew_ yet.

28 They forced the poor to cry out to God,
and he heard their calls for help.

29 If God decided to do nothing at all,
no one could criticize him.
If he hid his face, men would be helpless.
30 There would be nothing that nations could
do
to keep oppressors from ruling them.

31 Job, have you confessed your sins to God,
and promised not to sin again?
32 Have you asked God to show you your
faults,
and have you agreed to stop doing evil?
33 Since you object to what God does,
can you expect him to do what you
want?
It is your decision, not mine;
tell us now what you think.

34 Any sensible person will surely agree;
any wise man who hears me will say
35   that Job is speaking from ignorance,
and that nothing he says makes sense.
36 Think through everything that Job says;
you will see that he talks like an evil
man.
37 He refuses to stop sinning;
in front of us all he mocks and insults
God.

35 1-2 It is not right, Job, for you to say
that you are innocent in God's sight,
3 or to ask God, "How does my sin affect
you?
It has done me no good not to sin."

⁴ I am going to answer you and your friends
    too.

⁵ Look at the sky! See how high the clouds
        are!
⁶ If you sin, that does no harm to God.
        If you do many wrongs, does that affect
        him?
⁷ Do you help God by being so righteous?
        There is nothing God needs from you.
⁸ It is your fellow-men who suffer from your
        sins,   ,
        and the good you do helps them.

⁹ When men are oppressed they groan;
        they cry for someone to save them.
¹⁰   But they don't turn to God, their Crea-
        tor,
        who gives them strength in their darkest
        hours.
¹¹ They don't turn to God, who makes us
        wise,
        wiser than any animal or bird.
¹² They cry for help, but God doesn't an-
        swer,
        because they are proud and evil men.
¹³ It is useless for them to cry out;
        Almighty God does not see or hear
        them.

¹⁴ Job, you say you can't see God,
        but wait patiently—your case is before
        him.
¹⁵ You think that God does not punish,
        that he pays no attention to sin.
¹⁶ It is useless for you to go on talking;
        it is clear you don't know what you are
        saying.

36

Elihu

Elihu went on talking.

 ² Be patient and listen a little longer
  to what I am saying on God's behalf.
³ My knowledge is wide; I will use what I
    know
    to show that God, my Creator, is just.
⁴ Nothing I say to you is false;
    you see before you a truly wise man.

⁵ How strong God is! He despises no one;
    there is nothing he doesn't understand.
⁶ He does not let sinners live on,
    and he always treats the poor with jus-
      tice.
⁷ He protects those who are righteous;
    he lets them rule like kings,
    and lets them be honored forever.
⁸ But if people are bound in chains,
    suffering for what they have done,
⁹   God shows them their sins and their
      pride.
¹⁰ He makes them listen to his warning
    to turn away from evil.
¹¹ If they obey God and serve him,
    they live out their lives in peace and
      prosperity.
¹² But if not, they will die in ignorance
    and go to the world of the dead.

¹³ Those who are godless keep on being
      angry,
    and even when punished, they don't
      pray for help.
¹⁴ They die while they still are young,
    worn out by a life of disgrace.
¹⁵ But God teaches men through suffering
    and uses distress to open their eyes.

¹⁶ God brought you out of trouble,
and let you enjoy security;
your table was piled high with food.
¹⁷ But now you are getting the punishment
you deserve.^x
¹⁸ Be careful not to let bribes deceive you
and not to let riches lead you astray.
¹⁹ It will do you no good to cry out for help;
all your strength can't help you now.
²⁰ Don't wish for night to come,
the time when nations will perish.
²¹ Be careful not to turn to evil;
your suffering was sent to keep you
from it.

²² Remember how great is his power;
God is the greatest teacher of all.
²³ No one can tell God what to do
or accuse him of having done evil.
²⁴ God has always been praised for what he
does;
you also must praise him.
²⁵ Everyone has seen what he has done;
but no one understands it all.
²⁶ We cannot fully know God's greatness
or count the number of his years.

²⁷ It is God who takes water from the earth
and turns it into drops of rain.
²⁸ He lets the rain pour from the clouds
in showers for all mankind.
²⁹ No one knows how the clouds move,
or how the thunder roars through the
sky.
³⁰ He sends lightning through all the sky,
but the depths of the sea remain dark.
³¹ This is how he feeds^y the people
and provides an abundance of food.
³² He seizes the lightning with his hands,
and commands it to hit the mark.
³³ Thunder announces the approaching storm,
and the cattle know it is coming.

x *Verse 17 in Hebrew is unclear.* y feeds; *Hebrew* judges.

37 The storm makes my heart beat wildly.
² Listen, all of you, to the voice of God,
    to the thunder that comes from his
    mouth.
³ He sends the lightning across the sky;
    from one end of the earth to the other.
⁴ Then the roar of his voice is heard,
    the majestic sound of thunder,
    and all the while, the lightning flashes.
⁵ At God's command amazing things hap-
    pen,
    wonderful things that we can't under-
    stand.
⁶ He commands snow to fall on the earth,
    and sends torrents of drenching rain.
⁷ He brings the work of men to a stop;
    he made them; he shows them that he
    is at work.
⁸ The wild animals go to their dens and stay.
⁹ The storm winds come from the south,
    and the biting cold from the north.
¹⁰ The breath of God freezes the waters,
    and turns them to solid ice.
¹¹ Lightning flashes from the clouds,*
¹²   which circle about, obeying God's will.
    They do all that God commands,
    everywhere throughout the world.
¹³ God sends rain to water the earth;
    he may send it to punish men,
    or to show them his favor.

¹⁴ Pause a moment and listen, Job;
    consider the wonderful things God does.
¹⁵ Do you know how God gives a command
    and makes lightning flash from the
    clouds?
¹⁶ Do you know how clouds float in the sky,
    the work of God's amazing skill?
¹⁷ No, you can only suffer in the heat,
    when the south wind oppresses the land.
¹⁸ Can you help God stretch out the sky
    and make it as hard as polished metal?

* clouds; *Hebrew unclear.*

19 Teach us what to say to God;
    our minds are blank; we have nothing
      to say.
20 I won't ask God to let me speak;
    why should I give him a chance to de-
      stroy me?

21 And now the light in the sky is dazzling,
    too bright for us to look at it;
    and the sky has been swept clean by the
      wind.
22 A golden glow is seen in the north,
    and the glory of God fills us with fear.
23 God's power is so great that we cannot
      come near him;
    he is righteous and just in his dealings
      with men.
24 No wonder, then, that everyone fears him,
    and that he ignores those who claim to
      be wise.

The Lord Answers Job

38 Then out of the storm, the Lord spoke to Job.

The Lord

2 Who are you to question my wisdom?
    You are only showing your ignorance.
3 Stand up now like a man
    and answer the questions I am going to
      ask.
4 Were you there when I made the world?
    If you know so much, tell me about it.
5 Who decided how large it would be?
    Who stretched the measuring line over
      it?
    You know all this, don't you?
6 What holds up the pillars*a* that support
      the earth?
    Who laid the cornerstone of the world?

a PILLARS: See 9.6.

⁷ In the dawn of that day the stars sang to-
    gether,
    and the sons of God^b shouted for joy.

⁸ Who closed the gates to hold back the sea,^c
    when it burst from the womb of the
    earth?
⁹ It was I who covered the sea with clouds
    and wrapped it in darkness.
¹⁰ I marked^d a boundary for the sea
    and kept it behind bolted gates.
¹¹ I told it, "This far and no farther!
    Here your powerful waves must stop."
¹² Job, have you ever in all your life
    commanded a day to dawn?
¹³ Have you ordered the dawn to seize the
    earth
    and shake the wicked from their hiding
    places?
¹⁴ Daylight makes the hills and valleys stand
    out
    like the folds of a garment.
¹⁵ The light of day is too bright for the
    wicked,
    and prevents them from doing violence.

¹⁶ Have you been to the springs in the depths
    of the sea?
    Have you walked on the floor of the
    ocean?
¹⁷ Has anyone ever showed you the gates
    that guard the dark world of the dead?^e
¹⁸ Do you have any idea how big the world
    is?
    Answer me, if you know all this.

¹⁹ Do you know where the light comes from,
    or what the source of darkness is?

20 Can you show them how far to go,
   or send them back again?
21 I am sure you can, because you're so old,
   and were already born when the world
   was created.

22 Have you ever visited the storerooms,
   where I keep the snow and the hail?
23 I keep them ready for times of trouble,
   for days of battle and war.
24 Have you been to where the sun comes up,
   or the place from which the east wind
   blows?

25 Who dug a channel for the pouring rain,
   and cleared the way for the thunder-
   storm?
26 Who makes rain fall where no one lives?
27 Who waters the dry and thirsty land,
   so that grass springs up?
28 Does either the rain or the dew have a
   father?
29 Who is the mother of the ice and the
   frost,
30   which turn the waters to stone
   and freeze the face of the sea?

31 Can you tie the Pleiades[f] together,
   or loosen the bonds that hold Orion?[g]
32 Can you guide the stars season by season,
   and direct the Big and the Little
   Dipper?[h]
33 Do you know the laws that govern the
   skies,
   and can you make them apply to the
   earth?

---

[f] PLEIADES: See 9.9. [g] ORION: See 9.9. [h] THE BIG AND THE LITTLE
DIPPER: Two groups of stars resembling water dippers, also known as
Ursa Major and *Ursa Minor*, "Great Bear" and "Little Bear."

³⁴ Can you shout orders to the clouds,
   and make them drench you with rain?
³⁵ And if you command the lightning to
      flash,
   will it come to you and say, "At your
      service"?
³⁶ Who tells the ibisⁱ when the Nile will
      flood,
   or who tells the rooster^j that rain will
      fall?^k
³⁷ Who is wise enough to count the clouds,
   and tilt them over to send the rain,
³⁸   rain that hardens the dust into lumps?

³⁹ Do you find food for lions to eat,
   and satisfy hungry young lions,
⁴⁰   when they hide in their caves,
   or lie in wait in their dens?
⁴¹ Who is it that feeds the ravens
   when they wander about hungry,
   when their young cry to me for food?

---

i IBIS: A bird in ancient Egypt that was believed to announce the flooding of the Nile River. *j* ROOSTER: The rooster was thought to be able to predict the coming of rain. *k Verse 36 in Hebrew is unclear.*

39 Do you know when mountain goats are born?
Have you watched wild deer give birth?

2 Do you keep track of the months,
and know the time when their young will be born?

3 Do you know when they will crouch down
and bring their young into the world?

4 In the wilds their young grow strong;
they go away and don't come back.

5 Who gave the wild donkeys their freedom?
Who turned them loose and let them roam?

6 I gave them the desert to be their home,
and let them live on the salt plains.

7 They keep away from the noisy cities
and no one can tame them and make them work.

8 The mountains are the pastures where they feed,
where they search for anything green to eat.

9 Will a wild buffalo work for you?
Is he willing to spend the night in your stable?

10 Can you hold one with a rope and make him plow?
Or make him pull a harrow*l* in your fields?

11 Can you rely on his great strength
and expect him to do your heavy work?

12 Do you expect him to bring in your harvest,
and gather the grain from your threshing floor?

13 How fast the wings of an ostrich beat!
But no ostrich can fly like a stork.*m*

---

l HARROW: A farm implement used to level off the ground after plowing. *m* Verse 13 in Hebrew is unclear.

¹⁴ The ostrich leaves her eggs on the ground
    for the heat in the soil to warm them.
¹⁵ She is unaware that a foot may crush them
    or a wild animal break them.
¹⁶ She acts as if the eggs were not hers,
        and is unconcerned that her efforts are
        wasted.
¹⁷ It was I who made her foolish
    and did not give her wisdom.
¹⁸ But when she begins to run,ⁿ
    she can laugh at any horse and rider.

¹⁹ Was it you, Job, who made horses so
        strong,
    and gave them their flowing manes?
²⁰ Did you make them leap like locusts
    and frighten men with their snorting?
²¹ They eagerly paw the ground in the valley;
        they rush into battle with all their
        strength.
²² They do not know the meaning of fear,
    and no sword can turn them back.
²³ The weapons which their riders carry
    rattle and flash in the sun.
²⁴ Trembling with excitement, the horses
        race ahead;
    when the trumpet blows they can't stand
        still.
²⁵ At each blast of the trumpet they snort;
        they can smell a battle before they get
        near,
    and they hear the officers shouting com-
        mands.

²⁶ Does a hawk learn from you how to fly
        when it spreads its wings toward the
        south?
²⁷ Does an eagle wait for your command
    to build its nest high in the mountains?
²⁸ It makes its home on the highest rocks
    and makes the sharp peaks its fortress.

ⁿ run; *Hebrew unclear.*

29 From there it watches near and far
for something to kill and eat.
30 Around dead bodies the vultures gather,
and the young vultures drink the blood.

40

The Lord
1-2 Job, you challenged Almighty God;
will you give up now, or will you
answer?

Job
3-4 I spoke foolishly, Lord. What can I
answer?
I will not try to say anything else.
5 I have already said more than I should.

6 Then out of the storm the Lord spoke to Job again.

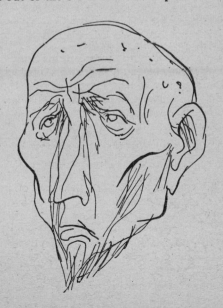

The Lord

7 Stand up now like a man,
and answer my questions.
8 Are you trying to prove that I am unjust—
to condemn me and put yourself in the right?
9 Are you as strong as I am?
Can your voice thunder as loud as mine?
10 If so stand up in your honor and pride;
clothe yourself with majesty and glory.
11 Look at those who are proud;
pour out your anger and humble them.
12 Yes, look at them and bring them down;
crush the wicked where they stand.
13 Bury them all in the ground;
bind them in the world of the dead.[o]
14 Then I will be the first to praise you,
and admit that you won the victory yourself.

15 Look at the monster Behemoth;[p]
I created him and I created you.
He eats grass like an ox,
16 but what strength there is in his body,
and what power there is in his muscles!
17 His tail stands up like a cedar,
and the muscles in his legs are strong.
18 His bones are as strong as bronze,
and his legs are like iron bars.

19 The most amazing of all my creatures!
Only his Creator can defeat him.
20 From the mountains where the wild beasts play,
grass is brought to feed him.[q]

[o] WORLD OF THE DEAD: See 10.21. [p] BEHEMOTH: An imaginary monster, sometimes identified with the hippopotamus. [q] *Verse 20 in Hebrew is unclear.*

21 He lies down under the thorn trees,
 and hides among the reeds in the swamp.
22 The thorn trees and the willows by the stream
 give him shelter in their shadows.
23 He is not afraid of a rushing river,
 he is calm when the water dashes in his face.
24 Who can blind his eyes and capture him?
 Or who can catch his snout in a trap?

41 Can you catch Leviathan[r] with a fishhook,
 or tie his tongue down with a rope?
2 Can you put a rope through his snout,
 or put a hook through his jaws?
3 Will he beg you to let him go?
 Will he plead with you for mercy?
4 Will he make an agreement with you
 and promise to serve you forever?
5 Will you treat him like a pet bird,
 like something to amuse your servant girls?
6 Will fishermen bargain over him?
 Will merchants cut him up to sell?
7 Can you fill his hide with fishing spears,
 or pierce his head with a harpoon?
8 Touch him once and you'll never try it again;
 you'll never forget the fight!

9 Anyone who sees Leviathan
 loses courage and falls to the ground.
10 When he is aroused, he is fierce;
 no one would dare to stand before him.
11 Who can attack him and still be safe?
 No one in all the world can do it.[s]

r LEVIATHAN: See 3.8. s *Verse 11 in Hebrew is unclear.*

¹² Let me tell you about Leviathan's legs,
    and describe how great and strong*t* he is.
¹³ No one can tear off his outer coat,
    or pierce the armor*u* he wears.
¹⁴ Who can make him open his jaws,
    ringed with those terrifying teeth?
¹⁵ His back*v* is made of rows of shields,
    fastened together and hard as stone.
¹⁶ Each one is fastened so tight to the next,
    not even a breath can come between.
¹⁷ They are all fastened so well together
    that nothing can ever pull them apart.
¹⁸ Light flashes when he sneezes,
    and his eyes glow like the rising sun.
¹⁹ Flames blaze from his mouth,
    and streams of sparks fly out.
²⁰ Smoke comes pouring out of his nose,
    like smoke from weeds burning under a
    pot.
²¹ His breath starts fires burning;
    flames leap out of his mouth.
²² His neck is so powerful
    that everyone who meets him is terrified.
²³ There is not a weak spot in his skin;
    it is as hard and unyielding as iron.
²⁴ His stony heart is without fear,
    as unyielding and hard as a millstone.
²⁵ When he rises up, even the gods are fright-
    ened;
    they are helpless with fear.
²⁶ There is no sword that can wound him;
    no spear, or arrow, or lance that can
    harm him.
²⁷ For him, iron is as weak as straw,
    and bronze as weak as rotten wood.
²⁸ There is no arrow that can make him run;
    rocks thrown at him are like bits of
    straw.
²⁹ To him a club is a piece of straw,
    and he laughs when men throw spears.

t how great and strong; *Hebrew unclear.* *u One ancient translation*
armor; *Hebrew* bridle. *v Some ancient translations* back; *Hebrew* pride.

30 His claws are like jagged pieces of pottery;
   they tear up the muddy ground as he
   walks.
31 He churns up the sea like a boiling pot,
   and makes it bubble like a kettle of oil.
32 He leaves a shining path behind him
   and turns the sea to white foam.
33 There is nothing on earth to compare with
   him;
   he is a creature that has no fear.
34 He looks down on even the proudest animals;
   he is king of all wild beasts.

42
Job

Then Job answered the Lord.

2 I know, Lord, that you are all-powerful;
   that you can do everything you want.
3 You ask how I dare question your wisdom
   when I am so very ignorant.
   I talked about things I did not understand,
   about marvels too great for me to know.
4 You told me to listen while you spoke
   and to try to answer your questions.
5 Then I knew only what others had told
   me,
   but now I have seen you with my own
   eyes;
6   so I am ashamed of all I have said
   and repent in dust and ashes.

CONCLUSION

⁷After the Lord had said all this to Job, he told Eliphaz, "I am angry with you and your two friends, because you did not speak the truth about me, the way my servant Job did. ⁸ Now take seven bulls and seven rams to Job and offer them as a sacrifice for yourselves. Job will pray for you, and I will answer his prayer and not disgrace you the way you deserve. You did not speak the truth about me as he did."

⁹ Eliphaz, Bildad, and Zophar did what the Lord had told them to do, and the Lord answered Job's prayer.

¹⁰ Then, after Job had prayed for his three friends, the Lord made him prosperous again and gave him twice as much as he had had before. ¹¹ All Job's brothers and sisters and former friends came to visit him and feasted with him in his house. They expressed their sympathy and comforted him for all the troubles the Lord had brought on him. Each of them gave him some money and a gold ring.

¹² The Lord blessed the last part of Job's life even more than he had blessed the first. Job owned 14,000 sheep, 6,000 camels, 2,000 head of cattle, and 1,000 donkeys. ¹³ He was the father of seven sons and three daughters. ¹⁴ He called the oldest daughter Jemimah, the second Keziah, and the youngest Keren-Happuch.ʷ ¹⁵ There were no other women in the whole world as beautiful as Job's daughters. Their father gave them a share of the inheritance along with their brothers.

¹⁶ Job lived 140 years after this, long enough to see his grandchildren and great-grandchildren. ¹⁷ And then he died at a very great age.

ʷ In Hebrew the names of Job's daughters suggest beauty both by their pleasing sound and by their meaning. *Jemimah* means "Dove"; *Keziah* means "Cassia," a variety of cinnamon used as a perfume; and *Keren-Happuch* means a small box for eye make-up.